# Worship Matters

## A Study for Congregations

JANE ROGERS VANN

WESTMINSTER
JOHN KNOX PRESS
LOUISVILLE · KENTUCKY

*First edition*
Published by Westminster John Knox Press
Louisville, Kentucky

11 12 13 14 15 16 17 18 19 20—10 9 8 7 6 5 4 3 2 1

*Book design by Sharon Adams*
*Cover design by Pam Poll Graphic Design*
*Cover art © Design Pics/SuperStock*

**Library of Congress Cataloging-in-Publication Data**

Vann, Jane Rogers, 1945–
    Worship matters : a study for congregations / Jane Rogers Vann.
        p. cm.
    ISBN 978-0-664-23416-4 (alk. paper)
    1. Public worship—Textbooks.   I. Title.
    BV15.V36   2010
    264—dc22

                                            2010034963

PRINTED IN THE UNITED STATES OF AMERICA

♾ The paper used in this publication meets the minimum requirements
of the American National Standard for Information Sciences—Permanence
of Paper for Printed Library Materials, ANSI Z39.48-1992.

Westminster John Knox Press advocates the responsible use of our natural resources.
The text paper of this book is made from at least 30% postconsumer waste.

# Contents

# Preface

*I*n the book of Revelation, John describes an image where absolutely every creature on land and sea sings praise to God at the same time and with one voice:

> To the one seated on the throne and to the Lamb
> be blessing and honor and glory and might
> forever and ever!
>
> (5:13)

That's just what we do when we gather for worship. A familiar prayer states, "We join our voices with prophets, apostles, and martyrs and with all the faithful in every time and place who forever sing to the glory of your name."

Doesn't it seem odd, then, that most congregations spend very little time talking about worship? It is *the* central act of the Christian faith. Our silence about worship has serious consequences. People become unsure about what they are doing in worship and why. It makes conversations about our spiritual lives difficult. Many Christians have the impression that spiritual matters are strictly individual and personal rather than shared in the community of faith. Most serious of all, the church's silence dulls our ability to discern God's presence in worship.

Worship invites a congregation into God's presence through many elements: people, space, furnishings, the arts, symbolic objects, music, words, actions. These many elements are often called the "languages" of worship. The languages of worship are symbolic rather than literal ones. For example, we recognize a worship space by its shape, size, and layout rather than by any sign declaring it a church. The space itself becomes a symbol for the worship of God. Another example is the words we use in worship. The language of Scripture is largely the language of metaphor and image, where the words point beyond themselves to deeper meanings. Look again at the passage from Revelation as this chapter begins. It describes God as the One on the "throne." No one knows, of course, whether or not God actually sits on a throne, but the image communicates God's greatness in terms that humans can understand. All of worship's languages work this way. In sight, sound, taste, touch, smell, and action, along with words, they communicate to us knowledge of God and ourselves that we could not otherwise understand. When congregations haven't been introduced to these languages and the ways they relate to one another, it is difficult to discern God's presence through them.

Imagine what might happen if congregations were encouraged to notice and seek to understand all of worship's many languages. Think what difference it would make if congregations grew in their ability to worship with eyes, ears, bodies, minds, and hearts wide open, anticipating and expecting the presence of God . . . and then to talk about it! The more worshipers enter wholeheartedly into worship, with its generous array of moods and actions, and the more they gather to ponder worship's meaning for their lives, the more thoroughly worshipers will find themselves joining heaven's unending songs of praise.

## Getting the Conversation Started

The purpose of this book is to provide resources for conversations that can support congregations and their leaders in their search for a deeper discernment of God's presence. Like many educators, I want to claim that all of the Christian life is a process of action and reflection.[1] The process of experience and reflection seems to be part of our human DNA. We humans are experiential beings who take in the world "whole" and then set about to figure out what our experiences are all about. We are *storytelling, pattern-seeking, meaning-making* beings. We participate in both special and everyday activities. We recall and reflect on those activities, searching for patterns. We connect new experiences with what has happened in the past. We also connect our experiences to the experiences of others, people we know well and people we meet in history, literature, Scripture, theology, and more. We tell our stories back to ourselves and to others as we "make meaning" that informs who we are. And then we anticipate some future experience in which we might participate, equipped with new understanding of what might be.

Although this process is natural to humans, why don't we use it when thinking about worship? There are many complex reasons for this. Yet ongoing conversations about worship could have incredible effects on our life together. Worship is, after all, the central defining act of the church. Conversations about worship are well worth our time and effort!

Conversations about worship require at least three things. First, congregations need to find suitable occasions for these conversations. And here the possibilities are richly varied and already exist in most congregations. They include groups of worship leaders such as choirs, ushers, lectors, acolytes, and eucharistic ministers; committee meetings, beginning-with-worship committees, altar guilds, and worship planning teams; teachers of children, youth, and adults and the classes they teach; and programmatic events such as circle meetings, luncheon programs, mom's-day-out programs, weeknight suppers, and so forth. Leaders can use these gatherings as opportunities to enter into conversations about worship in ways that will deepen the spiritual discernment of the whole congregation. Settings must provide a supportive environment that helps participants avoid the friction often associated with worship wars while at the same time facilitating straight talk about worship. Such an environment is marked by respectful listening, graceful questioning, and honest communication. Clear directions, wise leadership, and plenty of time are essential. When this way of talking together becomes commonplace in a congregation, all conversations, including conversations about worship, are more likely to occur.

Second, congregations need a set of categories that open them to a fuller examination of worship's many features. Sometimes worshipers become so accustomed to their congregation's way of doing things that they fail to notice the details. Social scientists often recommend "making the strange familiar and making the familiar strange." When we encounter communities whose practices are strange or new to us, we are called to become more familiar with them and to understand things from their point of view, from the inside. Thus we make the strange familiar. Likewise, when we make the familiar strange, we take the perspective of newcomers and strangers and view "the way we've always done it" with fresh eyes. This is not easy, so it is helpful to separate our worship practices into more manageable bits. Social scientists are again helpful in offering us categories they have found useful when studying rituals in worldwide contexts. These categories include the *space* for worship and the ways the space is decorated and used; the *time* for worship, including the ways in which hours, days, and seasons are marked; the *actions* of worship—who does what when; the ways *language* is used in worship; and the use of *music* in worship. Thinking of these as the "languages" of worship helps us understand worship as an *event in which we participate* rather than a series of texts to be read. They help us notice how worship is carried out and how participants engage in the event itself.

In his list of "maxims for planning of Christian Rituals," Tom Driver declares that "Ritual loves not paper."[2] Rather, he says, worship is about *doing something*, about using our bodies and voices to call upon God and offer ourselves, body and soul, to the Creator of heaven and earth. It is this *event* quality, this *doing*, that deserves our attention. Rather than focus on analyzing the texts in the Sunday bulletin or on our own response, we are able to broaden our perspectives to include the many elements that make worship an event and the ways these elements interact with one another. While each of the languages of worship communicates an indispensable aspect of worship, "the liturgy is meant to speak to us as one total language, richly and harmoniously varied. It seeks to evoke in us an experience of ourselves as God's people. We do [well], then, to think of each sensory language as a unique and valuable way in which . . . experience is opened up to us in harmony with all the other languages being used."[3] Recognizing, understanding, and asking questions about these languages outside of worship encourages worshipers to discern God's voice through the multiple languages of worship.

Third, congregations need skills in asking the right question at the right time. Learning the Christian life from the experience of congregational life requires participation and reflection. A central strategy for initiating and sustaining reflection is the asking of carefully crafted questions and allowing plenty of time for exploring possible responses. Not all reflection is the same, so surely not all questions are the same. A pattern of *description* of past events, *analysis* of those events in light of Scripture and tradition, and opportunities to *imagine and plan* for future events—these form a pervasive pattern in human learning. There are times when reflection consists of recall and exploration of past experience in all its multifaceted complexity. Questions might include "Describe what you heard, saw, touched, felt. . . ." At other times careful analysis is required as meaning is being distilled. Here we need questions like "How does this story from Scripture compare with our experience of . . . ?" When we are looking into the future, imagining what a future event might be like, we need questions like "What hopes do we have for the coming season of . . . ?" and "How would that hope be embodied and enacted in our worship?" At each chapter's end, the questions for discussion are organized in this way. Each set of questions is introduced by an "Ideal" that describes some aspect of worship. Then participants are asked to "describe" some aspect of worship, to "explain how" they are affected by it, and to "imagine" worship in the future. The pattern provides a structured but flexible template for open, honest, constructive conversations. No one conversation could make use of all the questions provided in the following chapters. Choose two or three questions that are especially fitting for your congregation, and come back to the rest at another time. Try to include a question from each category: *describe, analyze, imagine, and plan.*

Inspiration for this book comes from two sources. One source is the congregations I visit and have belonged to that nurture my own liturgical spiritual formation. In congregations, Christians are formed and take on the likeness of Christ. People of faith are hungry for encounters with God in their congregations and for ways more thoroughly to absorb and be changed by those encounters. It is for these congregations that I write.

The other source of inspiration for this book is Gilbert Ostdiek's classic text *Catechesis for Liturgy: A Program for Parish Involvement.*[4] I have used this book, written for Roman Catholic congregations in the midst of liturgical renewal, for over ten years. As extensive experimentation in mainline denominations begins to mature and we reflect critically on what we have learned, it is my hope that this book for Protestant congregations will serve purposes similar to those offered to Catholic congregations by Ostdiek.

I have spent time in congregations across the mainline Protestant spectrum in order to "overhear" the conversations these congregations are having, with hopes that as readers listen in, they will be inspired with a vision for conversations in their own congregations. Congregations were chosen according to three criteria. They take worship seriously and place it at the center of their life together. They are healthy congregations that have stable pastoral, musical, and educational leadership. Conversations about worship are a regular part of their congregational culture. Yet they want more! Over and over during the course of this research, members of congregations and their leaders, even those who were already talking fruitfully about worship, told me that they would love to talk more about worship but they did not know how to go about it. They were stymied by the conditions of congregational life that inhibit conversations and are eager for strategies for overcoming some of these obstacles.

A spirit of hospitality was pervasively present in all these congregations. In these congregations I found groups of faithful Christians who talk openly and creatively about the presence of God in worship and their efforts more fully to discern and respond to that presence. My heartfelt thanks go to the members, lay leaders, musicians, and pastors of Little River United Church of Christ, Annandale, Virginia; ChristChurch Presbyterian, Bellaire, Texas; Saint Stephen's Episcopal Church, Richmond, Virginia; Grace Episcopal Church, Newton Corner, Massachusetts; Christ Lutheran Church, Richmond, Virginia; Tustin Presbyterian Church, Tustin, California; Spanish Springs Presbyterian Church, Sparks, Nevada; Saint Luke's Lutheran Church, Park Ridge, Illinois; Bethlehem Lutheran Church, Saint Cloud, Minnesota; and First Congregational United Church of Christ, Asheville, North Carolina.

This book is written with the hope that new and fruitful conversations will ignite congregations in both the depth of their own worship and the breadth of their invitation to others to join them in the worship of God. Chapter 1 explores some of the reasons congregations don't talk about worship and proposes strategies for overcoming this reluctance. Chapter 2 examines the languages of worship and their symbolic ways of communicating. Chapters 3 through 8 examine each liturgical language, drawing on denominational documents and on the worship life of congregations for its descriptions. It is hoped that conversations inspired by these chapters will allow congregations to reflect critically on their worship and affirm those practices that bring honor to God and form the assembly into the people of God.[5]

Research in these congregations has been generously supported by the sabbatical and faculty support provisions at Union Theological Seminary and Presbyterian School of Christian Education. In addition, further support has come from a grant from the Calvin Institute of Christian Worship. Special thanks go to Betty Grit and John Witvliet for their encouragement and wise counsel. Thanks go most of all to my husband, Dan, who proved to be an excellent travel agent, traveling companion, and copy editor.

Chapter 1

# Not Talking about Worship

*T*he sanctuary of Saint Luke's Lutheran Church in Park Ridge, Illinois, is festively decked in red—table covering, paraments, banners—as Pastors Stephen Larson and Kristi Weber and I sit and talk about the worship life of the congregation. The pastors, educators, musicians, and lay leaders at Saint Luke's are a great team! They work collaboratively, cumulatively, and intentionally as they invite the congregation—young and old, newcomers and longtime members, leaders and pew sitters—into the presence of God each Lord's Day. So I am more than a little surprised that as we conclude our conversation the pastors turn to one another and say, "Gee, we've never really talked about worship like this together, have we?" In the midst of all their excellent collaboration, conversations about worship seldom go below the surface. As I begin a similar conversation with two longtime lay leaders at Little River United Church of Christ just outside Washington, D.C., I hear something of the same sentiment. Jane Hustveldt says, "Talk about worship? What's to talk about? The service is the service!"

Imagine you are with my friends Chip and Paul as they conclude worship at a regional conference and move to a seminar titled "Worship Reflections." The conference is focused on exploring the seasons of Holy Week, Easter, and Pentecost, and the seminar is a place where participants are invited to explore more deeply the worship events in which they have just participated. Chip and Paul, both experienced pastors and worship leaders, introduce themselves and invite the group to begin their conversation together by naming images and metaphors they recall from the morning's "Easter" service. To their surprise, most of the comments bypass this invitation to explore the metaphorical languages of worship and focus instead on aspects of worship that trivialize worship's intention of inviting encounter with God ("I didn't like the place of the announcements in the service nor the way they were done").

1

It seems that Christians don't talk much about worship and, if they do, they confine their conversations to a narrow range of, some would say, trivial topics. When I've asked members and leaders in congregations across the country to tell me about the conversations they have about worship, they often have a hard time recounting actual conversations, saying their congregation doesn't really talk about worship very much. The conversations they report reveal that it is easier to talk about the pragmatic aspects of worship—who will do what when—than it is to talk about the role of worship in the life of the congregation and its deep meaning for the gathered assembly. This seems odd, given the extensive changes in worship that have been introduced into mainline churches over the past twenty-five years or so. The life of the church is grounded in its worship of the living God. Week by week, season by season, year by year, the church faithfully assembles each Lord's Day to turn its undivided attention toward the creator of heaven and earth. Christians gather, bringing praise, thanksgiving, confession, lament, and intercession; engaging in singing, dancing, storytelling, washing, eating, and drinking. How is it that Christians find nothing to talk about?

When people confess that they don't talk about worship, my next question always is, Why not? I've collected an interesting list of responses that point toward the need for more effective strategies to help congregations discuss the gathering that is the primary focus of their common life.

## Congregations don't talk about worship because . . .

### . . . people are too busy

Most active members of most congregations are very busy people. Try to schedule an extra meeting, and you will know what I mean. Because worship is important in the life of a congregation, conversations about it require careful attention, and that takes time. Rather than enter into such conversations in a halfhearted way, many members step back from engaged discussions about the liturgy and let others take care of things.

When the leaders of Grace Episcopal Church in Newton Corner, Massachusetts, faced this situation, the pastors and musician saw their best opportunities for conversation within gatherings that were already going on. At choir rehearsal every week, musician Linda Clark is quick to make theological and liturgical connections between the music the choir sings and its place in the liturgy. On a recent summer Sunday, Assistant Rector Ed Pease led an

Grace Episcopal Church choir, Newton Corner, Massachusetts, with Linda Clarke, director. Photo by Carol Robinson. Used with permission.

"instructed liturgy." As the community gathered to worship, each element of their celebration was explored theologically and liturgically, exposing its deeper meanings. Ed says he avoided a mechanical, practical explanation of the liturgy, opting for a deeper kind of exploration, with hopes that it would lead to congregation-wide meaning-making conversations. And it had the hoped-for outcome. In late fall when I visited them, the congregation was still talking about that Sunday, still exploring the liturgy's meaning for their ongoing life together.

### . . . Worship belongs to the pastor (and maybe the musicians)

Most mainline denominations have produced materials related to the liturgy during the past decade and have made strong systematic efforts to expand each congregation's participation in and understanding of their liturgical heritage and practice. Nevertheless the assumption persists that liturgy is something best left to the "professionals." It is easy for people to come to the conclusion that they *shouldn't* understand. People say they don't know

anything about worship so they shouldn't comment. They just want someone to tell them what to do. That's good enough. If they've gotten the message that worship belongs to pastors and musicians, they are not motivated
to become curious and ask questions, and that's too bad. It does make life
easier for pastors and musicians. It is easier and more efficient to plan worship themselves and leave the "amateurs" out of the process. Unfortunately
this keeps most lay leaders and members at arm's length from opportunities
for learning about the liturgy and from the kind of theological reflection it
engenders. And the people in the pews are quick to get the message that their
role is to become spectators and do what they are told.

In many congregations laypeople often take active parts in Lord's Day
worship, but without much preparation for their roles. I have said (loudly)
for decades that, as an educator, the task I would most gladly undertake in
my congregation would be to help prepare worship leaders—greeters, ushers, lectors, crucifers, acolytes, leaders of prayers—for their roles. Recently
I was able to work with my colleague Ronald Byars to help the lectors at our
church understand and carry out their role as readers of Scripture. We began
with prayer for the presence of the Holy Spirit and then moved to some of
the practical aspects of their ministry, but before long a conversation about
a theology of Scripture began to emerge, and the connections between these
lectors' tasks and their own spiritual formation were evident. These longtime
lay leaders had never before been given the opportunity to develop sufficient
confidence in their task so that its inherent spiritually formative qualities
could be explored. They were eager for the opportunity and grateful for the
spiritual fruit it could bear. The word *liturgy* means "the work of the people."
In order for this to become a reality for the church today, pastors, musicians,
lay leaders, and all other members are called to share responsibility for worship in new and different ways that include preparation, full participation,
and reflection on their roles.

### . . . Worship leaders don't want questions

I've known congregations, and perhaps you've known them too, where pastoral, educational, and/or musical leadership is not receptive to questions
about worship. Sometimes leaders are distracted by other issues or programs.
Perhaps they view such questions as a challenge to their authority. It may be
that leaders make some of the same assumptions as members of congregations, assumptions reflected in this list. Whatever the cause, there are subtle
signals that let members of congregations know that their questions about
worship are not welcome.

### . . . Worship is too controversial

Much has been written about the worship wars and congregational conflict centered around worship style. Many people have been left with the twin impressions that worship is all about style and that disagreements about style are much too painful to get into. These conflicts have taken place during one of the most broadly experimental periods of recent church history and have resulted in both heartbreak and spiritual deepening. Often liturgical experiments are initiated by small cliques of would-be worship leaders whose enthusiasm outstrips their understanding of the congregation's worshiping traditions. Those outside these cliques know from bitter experience that trying to talk through different hopes and expectations is risky indeed. Sometimes the only question people know to ask one another about worship is, "Did you like it?" This immediately makes worship a matter of personal preference. In my experience "Did you like it?" is the wrong question. Church architect E. A. Sövik takes note of this question, saying, "The questions some people put to themselves when they encounter a new architectural form, or any new art form, are, 'Do I like it? Does it please me?' The questions are the same as one asks oneself about a new flavor of ice cream or a new brand of cigar. . . . It cannot be right to judge Chartres Cathedral and a piece of pie by the same criteria."[1] One of the aims of this book is to offer different (better) questions to ask when inviting discussion about worship.

Christ Lutheran Church, Richmond, Virginia. New paraments, tablecloths, and banner. Photo by Dave Swager. Used with permission.

When the altar guild of Christ Lutheran Church in Richmond, Virginia, began to consider the worship environment of their church, they started with questions about the liturgical year: What are the origins and meanings of the liturgical seasons? What images and metaphors are found in the Scriptures read during each season? How might those images and metaphors become a part of our liturgical environment? What difference might their presence make for our worship? With these questions in mind, the altar guild held a lengthy conversation with a fabric artist and a theologian/biblical scholar. Out of that conversation the artist designed a tablecloth, paraments, and banner for the congregation to use during the season of Pentecost. The questions they asked had more to do with the centrality and meaning of the liturgy than with personal preference and opinion. Questions like these can lead to conversations about worship that bring controversial issues to light but help to avoid disagreements over likes and dislikes.

### . . . "Fad-o-phobia": Fear of blindly following the latest trends

When the contemporary and seeker-friendly worship styles emerged a couple of decades ago, congregations began a broad range of experiments, some of which were appropriate to their congregational life and heritage and some of which were not. Even people who were not opposed to such innovation were wary of just following current fads. Congregations and their leaders found themselves without adequate resources for charting the direction of changes in worship. Without opportunities for constructive conversations, experiments in many places were tried for a short time and then set aside as the congregation went back to its customary patterns.

At Saint Stephen's Episcopal Church in Richmond, worship traditions provide a stable foundation for a wide variety of experiments and innovations in worship, most notably a weekly Celtic evensong service. Within the ongoing life of this traditional congregation, a variety of kinds of music, liturgical action, storytelling, and prayer have been introduced. Pastors, musicians, and worship leaders draw on a broad range of resources, all the while staying within their own deep theological traditions. Thus their worship is always fresh and lively, never trendy or faddish.

### . . . We don't want to be labeled "narrow minded"

At the other end of the spectrum from the need to have worship "the way I like it" is the notion that only the narrow-minded are reluctant to accept innovative worship practices. Sometimes conversations about worship are

Saint Stephen's Episcopal Church, Richmond, Virginia. Baptismal font. Photo by Sarah Bartenstein. Used with permission.

First Congregational United Church of Christ, Asheville, North Carolina. Photo by Christopher Oakley. Used with permission.

undermined because of an implicit message that if someone else likes worship this way, who am I to disagree? Being a moderate or liberal congregation seems to mean "we accept everything."

At First Congregational United Church of Christ in Asheville, North Carolina, which recently moved into a historic downtown church building, conversations about worship began to center around inclusive language. For some time, members and leaders had been sensitive to issues of language in worship, but suddenly these issues began to take on heightened importance. When it came time for open, compassionate, honest conversation, the pastors invited the gathered participants to *tell stories*. They asked members, "Describe the times and places when you became aware of inclusive language as an important element of worship." "Tell us about those persons who have been important in shaping your understanding of inclusive language." These and questions like them led the group into a level of mutual understanding and generosity that allowed them to grapple constructively with more controversial aspects of inclusive language. Rather than "accept everything," they heard stories of how deep meaning is made and have come to respect differing viewpoints.

As a recent church advertisement puts it, the church is a "come as you are" but not a "stay as you are" kind of place. The church exists within a broad and deep stream of history where the purposes and practices of worship can be clearly discerned. Though there is generous latitude for variety and local practices, worship is not, at its heart, about personal preferences. Members of congregations are called to move beyond both polarization and giving in for the sake of personal preferences. Congregations are called to move toward worship's central norms, uniquely embodied in each community. In this book those central norms are expressed as "Ideals" at the end of each chapter and lead to questions for discussion.

### . . . The church has too many other concerns, and Worship is not at the top of the list

Every congregation must balance its activities with its energy and resources. There is usually more to do than the congregation can get done, so choices must be made and efficiencies must be introduced. Under these common circumstances, it is easy to set aside the demanding practice of talking about worship and focus the congregation's energies on more pressing needs. It is easy to "streamline" conversations so that precious time and energy can be spent elsewhere.

At Spanish Springs Presbyterian Church in Sparks, Nevada, an eight-year-old congregation meeting in a suburban strip mall storefront, careful allocation of energy would seem natural, given all that needs to be accomplished in this young congregation. But members of this congregation are hungry for conversations about worship. They understand its centrality to their life as a congregation, and they are eager to understand why their worship is different from the many megachurches that surround them. The energy they give to exploring the meaning of worship actually *increases* the energy they have for community outreach and mission.

### . . . There are not a lot of venues for talking about worship

Sometimes the places where one would expect to overhear probing conversations about worship turn out to be the last places where such conversations actually occur. I've been to many worship committee meetings, governing board meetings, and staff meetings where worship is discussed only in terms of its mechanics and logistics, with never a mention of worship's deeper meanings. For many of the reasons listed above, pastors, educators, and musicians are reluctant to create opportunities where a deeper level

Spanish Springs Presbyterian Church, Sparks, Nevada. Photo by Doug Ramseth. Used with permission.

of discussion might be possible, but the consequences of such avoidance are risky.

Bethlehem Lutheran Church in Saint Cloud, Minnesota, is notable for the eagerness with which adult and children's choirs, Sunday school classes for children and adults, arts committees, worship-planning teams, and families engage in serious study and conversations about the liturgy. These conversations—which happen around dinner tables, conference tables, and during musical rehearsals—demonstrate that conversations about worship need not be confined to special events and groups. Rather, worship is the central event that orients the life of the congregation. Conversations about a whole range of issues often circle back to this congregation's identity, first and foremost, as a worshiping community. There are regularly scheduled opportunities for talking about worship, and the conversations begun there spill over into other times and places.

### . . . We don't want to offend God

The separation between the sacred and secular, church and world, is sometimes so complete that the realities of life with God seem impossible to comprehend. How can it be that the very ordinariness, complexity, and difficulty of twenty-first-century life can bear the marks of God's presence? How can it be that the sacred mysteries of the church's worship are meant to be understood by "ordinary folk like me"? Christians are supposed to understand this stuff, right? Won't God be offended by my ignorance? What if I say the wrong thing? There may have been a time when all churchgoers understood the church's language, symbols, and metaphors, but I doubt it. And more to the point, human curiosity is God's gift. My historian husband says, "What everybody knows, nobody bothers to write down." For a long time now we have wrongly assumed that everybody knows what worship is and how to understand its multiple dimensions. For this reason, when I teach courses on the liturgy, I usually begin with an illustrated slide show on the history of the liturgy. When we know the origins and explanations for the ways we worship, we develop a keener ability to understand why we do what we do now. God is not offended by this kind of curiosity and investigation: it serves to deepen our discernment of God's abiding presence in the liturgy.

### . . . We must hide our doubts and theological struggles

A young mother of three looked at me and said frankly, "I like to come to church here because the sermons don't piss me off!" She had come through

Bethlehem Lutheran Church, Saint Cloud, Minnesota. Photo by Steve Cook. Used with permission.

more conservative congregations where the tension between her questions and the required faith response meant that she left church angry almost every Sunday. Her faith, she said, is "hanging by a thread most Sundays." Under these circumstances, conversations about the church's worship, where its deepest beliefs are acted out, puts a lot on the line. Her present congregation allows room for her doubts, questions, and expressions of struggle, so conversations about worship are much more natural and comfortable. Worship is intended to gather us before God in an environment that is honest about the human condition and about God's reconciling intentions for all creation. With this in mind, probing conversations about worship may indeed call for the reexamination of our most closely held beliefs. It is the intention of this book to help ensure that such reexaminations lead to the deepening and strengthening of faith, not its weakening. To suppress such conversations when "faith is hanging by a thread" sends the message that such doubts are unimportant and/or unwelcome—an attitude that can ultimately lead to breaking the thread of faith, not strengthening it.

Many of the reasons given by congregations for not talking about worship are valid and deserve our consideration. On the other hand, the official documents of all the denominations represented in this study—Episcopal, United Methodist, Presbyterian, Lutheran, United Church of Christ—indicate that worship is the central most important aspect of their ecclesial identity. Several of these denominations refer to the existence of the church as the place where "the gospel is purely preached and the holy sacraments are administered according to the gospel."[2] The Presbyterian *Book of Common Worship*, with which I am most familiar, was adopted "with the fervent prayer that [the new book] may be an effective aid to congregations as they worship God, and that it may further the renewal of the church's faith and life."[3] But declaring that worship is the center of the church's identity and life is not enough. The church must also organize and live out its common life in ways that reflect this orientation. Congregational life will need to move away from "fun stuff to do so people will like to come to church" and toward identifying and lifting up the ways every part of the congregation's life is related to its central communal action: the worship of God.

## Until All Creation Sings

Chapters 4 and 5 of Revelation offer a description of the cosmic worship of God that is even now under way. The central most important calling for Christians is to join with all creation to give praise and glory to God. It is this vision for the redemption of all creation that informs and inspires our worship. This central calling issues in two specific missions for the church: to *broaden* and *deepen* the worship of God. The church *broadens* the worship of God when it invites those who do not now give praise and glory to God to join us. Perhaps there are those who have not heard the stories of God's grace, so the church is called to tell those stories as an invitation to join the church's praise. Others may be unable to praise God because of oppression, poverty, grief, or illness. The church is called to ease human suffering in the name of Christ as an invitation to those in need to add their voices to the church's song. Likewise, the church is also called to *deepen* its own capacity to give ever more faithful and complete praise to God by an enriched life of prayer, study, companionship in Christ, careful self-examination, repentance, and discernment of God's grace. Committed, open conversations about what we do in worship and why we do it contribute to both these missions, so that one day *all creation will sing to the glory of God.*

Chapter 2

# The Symbolic Languages of Worship

*When we come to church, then, we see before us or near us bread, wine, and water. Even before their use, these things are already symbols—that is, they gather together many meanings in one focused place, giving us a means actually to participate in those meanings. They are already sacred—that is, among the meanings they suggest are elements of transcendence, of something larger than our circle.*

*Gordon Lathrop*[1]

*C*ongregations gladly struggle with the complexities of including children in worship precisely because they believe that we learn to worship by worshiping. And this is just as true for adults as it is for children. As an educator I am intrigued by the common sense of that claim and by the need to investigate it further. What are the processes we know as "learning"? What do we learn, and how? In worship, learning happens intentionally but indirectly. We learn to worship and to know God, ourselves, and our world in a uniquely Christian way through repeated participation in the community's weekly gathering around pulpit, font, and table. Long before Sunday schools (a relatively recent programmatic development in Christian history), Christians learned to worship by worshiping. In fact, when worship becomes dominated by instruction, its natural way of indirect learning is undercut. Rather, worship depends on the processes of memory, imagination, symbolic words, actions, and objects, all in an embodied, participatory setting. And the resulting learning is more than can be achieved through teaching and instruction. What a congregation learns is its own identity as a people of God through its undistracted attention to the presence of God, made known through symbolic words, actions, and objects. The symbolic languages of worship speak powerfully as the church gathers to focus all of its attention on the presence of God. In this chapter we will explore the ways the symbolic languages of

15

worship function, calling on memory and imagination through the use of ritual action and symbols. Toward the end of the chapter we will propose a way of thinking about the use of symbols as play.

## Memory and Imagination

At Bethlehem Lutheran Church in Saint Cloud, Minnesota, children are always welcome in worship. The space is large, and no one is disturbed by children's natural level of activity. At the Great Vigil of Easter, a two-hour service celebrated after dark on Easter Saturday, children take major roles. The Vigil includes as many as twelve lengthy Old Testament and New Testament readings that recount stories and, taken together, tell *The Story* of God's way with humankind. Associate Pastor Steve Cook, an avid storyteller himself, enlists dozens of children in telling and enacting these many stories. In the process of faithful engagement with biblical texts—learning the stories,

Bethlehem Lutheran Church, Saint Cloud, Minnesota. Photo by Steve Huss. Used with permission.

rehearsing, and enacting these stories—children and adults are drawn into remembering and participating in, maybe even reliving the stories and events that shape Christian faith. So the children and adults at Bethlehem Lutheran, through the storytelling of the Great Vigil of Easter, know themselves to be participants in this ancient yet ongoing story of God's own people.

Learning Christian faith in this way calls on both memory and imagination. We usually think of memory as a kind of reminiscence, recalling what has happened in the past. Recent research in brain science reveals something quite different, however. Memories, say brain scientists, are not the simple recall of past events. Rather, because of the way the brain is structured, with auditory memory stored in one part of the brain, visual memory in another, and emotional memory in yet another, memories are complex, active reconstructions of past events. Various components of past events are called to mind in ways that are heavily dependent on what is happening in the present. As a result the act of remembering brings events and stories of the past into the here and now.

In Christian worship, congregations are called upon to remember before God all that God has done and promised. In worship, in the very act of gathering on a Sunday morning, we call into active presence the deeds of God with the ancient Israelites, the preaching of prophets, the poetry of psalmists, and the life, death, and resurrection of Jesus Christ. According to Don Saliers,

> Seeking God and embodying holiness in our whole existence depends, in great measure, on receiving and exercising the memories of the Scriptures in and through particular forms of communal traditions. Living our lives open to God requires dwelling in a common history, the narratives, the writings of the prophets, the witness of the apostles, and the extended memories of the community praying and living in accordance with them through time.[2]

Without this shared memory, says Saliers, it would be impossible for Christians to live out their calling as the body of Christ. When adults and children participate in the stories of the Israelites crossing the sea on dry land or look with Ezekiel across the valley of dry bones, their memories are extended. When the people of Bethlehem Lutheran gather around the large, bubbling pool to renew their baptism, when they gather at the table to celebrate with bread and wine the life of the risen Christ in their midst, their memories are extended. The realities of their everyday lives as a community of faith and as individuals are brought into the presence of the risen One and are given new meaning through the extension of memory to include God's way with humankind.

Bethlehem Lutheran Church, Saint Cloud, Minnesota. Photo by author. Used with permission.

Thus the scriptural and sacramental memory bestowed in worship is, in the words of Saliers, "redemptive memory":

> What is true of our common experience as human beings—the joys and grief, the pity, despair, and hope—these deep emotions and abiding features of our common lot are to be given a new shape and a particular content. In worship, prayer, and the life of compassionate discipleship, remembering with the Scriptures over time and in all circumstances is to turn in a new direction. We live, feel, intend, and understand the world differently because a shared biblical memory forms us in an awareness and disposition oriented toward the mystery of God. Entering the patterns of redemptive memory with the people of God risks conversion.[3]

The people of Bethlehem Lutheran understand this well. Their present building is about fifteen years old and was built on the outskirts of town well before the surrounding neighborhoods were built. Their former building was located in the old downtown area and offered no possibilities for expanding to meet the needs of the growing congregation. The decision to

Bethlehem Lutheran Church, Saint Cloud, Minnesota. Photo by author. Used with permission.

build in a new location was difficult but was entered into with deep sensitivity to the memories residing in their historic church building. Pastor Dee Pederson recalls that as they prepared to move, memories were called into the present, honored, and included in the congregation's continuing identity. "Each week we gave thanks for the life-shaping activities of the old site— baptisms, marriages, confirmation, funerals. We made paper chains of all the names of those baptized there. On the final day we packed the candles, lectionary book, chalice. We worshiped outdoors on the farm site, the new location, with a trailer [loaded] with chairs. We unpacked the candles, lectionary book, and chalice. It was a M*A*S*H unit church." By treasuring the memory of God's abiding presence with them, the congregation was able to discern that continued abiding presence, even in a farmer's field where no building yet stood. Memory and imagination worked together to draw this congregation into the presence of God and to experience God's abiding presence, even as they faced a future filled with change. Their ability to remember and retell their history as God's people became a sign of the life of God in their midst.

For the people of Bethlehem Lutheran, confidence in God's abiding presence rested in treasured memories, to be sure. But it also called upon the ability to imagine, to see what was not yet present, and to engage in energized work toward what might be. By imagination I do not mean pretending. Rather, this kind of imagination is the ability to see beyond the limits of the material world in the here and now. It is the ability to discern connections between our own stories and the biblical story in what might be called imaginative discernment. According to Craig Dykstra, the artists among us may be the ones most able to describe this imaginative capacity, the ability to see into the future.

> Artists in every medium have an imagination and an intelligence that enables them to pull together what they perceive in the world and contemplate in their souls in the process of creating new works of art that in turn help the rest of us apprehend reality in entirely new ways. . . . This imagination relies on individual gifts but is also shaped by the community, education, artistic tradition and material relations within which the artist works over time.[4]

Dykstra calls this "seeing in depth." Worship invites us into this kind of seeing in depth. And according to the work of learning theorist Josh Waitzkin, "Depth beats breadth any day of the week, because it opens a channel for the intangible, unconscious, creative components of our hidden potential."[5] Part of learning to worship includes a kind of artistic sensitivity to the possibilities. Imaginative participation in the church's story with connections to our own story offers a depth of meaning that unites past, present, and future; community and individual; heart, mind, body, and soul.

## Ritual, Symbol, and Metaphor

The church's depth perception includes many kinds of stories, ritual actions, symbols, and metaphors drawn primarily from Scripture and the church's ancient traditions. Look around almost any Christian church: you will see furnishings, objects, and images in stained-glass windows that call to mind stories from Scripture and the history of the church. At Tustin Presbyterian Church, in Tustin, California, where the sanctuary has been newly remodeled, the stained-glass windows feature images of biblical characters, and high on the wall of the chancel is a window depicting the Good Shepherd. The pulpit, the eight-sided font, and table are engraved with wheat, grapes,

Tustin Presbyterian Church, Tustin, California. Photo by Helen Anderson. Used with permission.

and the trefoil, a symbol for the Trinity. The congregation's paraments, designed and collected over the course of several years, are in vivid reds, greens, purples, and white, which correspond to the seasons of the church year. They display images of a Holy Spirit dove, vine and branches, a Jesse Tree, and a lamb surrounded by a crown of thorns, among others. Banners adorn the sanctuary during festival seasons. Each Sunday, worship begins with water bearers, usually children or teenagers, processing up the center aisle and pouring water into the baptismal font, which sits front and center in the sanctuary. The images, colors, furnishings, ritual actions, and the words that accompany them serve to remind worshipers of the ongoing story of God's way with humankind and their place in that story.

Except for stained-glass windows, which have usually had a place in mainline Protestant houses of worship, the intentional recovery of color, symbol, and ritual action has been rather recent. Many Protestants have grown up with the notion that "ritual is nothing but a crutch for the intellectually weak."[6] Even so, it is a fact that all religious groups have rituals—patterns of

Tustin Presbyterian Church, Tustin, California. Photo by Helen Anderson. Used with permission.

speech, repeated actions, the order of events—that help to bear the group's identity. The familiarity, predictability, and relational context of ritual helps us know ourselves as "us." And as communications specialists have long reminded us, communication often depends more on context, gesture, and vocal inflection than on words themselves. So it is not a matter of having ritual or not. Rather, it is a matter of which ritual. Authentic ritual needs living symbols—words, actions, spaces, and objects that give expression to the assembly's intention to place themselves in God's presence and at the same time shape their discernment of the presence of the creator of heaven and earth.[7]

In chapter 1 we referred to the elements and dimensions of worship as "languages," pointing out the nonverbal nature of the majority of these liturgical languages. Worship is largely nonverbal, made up of gestures, postures, communal actions, and song. The words used in worship provide the context, reference points, and stories that make worship distinctively Christian.[8] The languages of worship include the size, design, lighting, and acoustics of the worship space itself as well as its furnishings and decorations. And the assembly and its leaders, their actions, gestures, songs, and words surely add their own languages. All of these languages contribute to the symbolic richness of Christian worship and convey more, much more, than words alone.

Maybe you have heard people say, as I have, that this or that is "merely symbolic." Although I think I understand what is being said, that the symbolic nature of some event or object means that it is of little or no consequence, this is *not* what we mean when we speak of the symbolic languages of Christian liturgy. Don Saliers says, "As with poetry and literature, the symbols in living liturgy mean more than they say, and they present to human beings much more than what appears. This is the nature of signs become symbols."[9]

It is helpful here to make a distinction between "signs" and "symbols." Signs and symbols both refer to things that are not directly given. The usual example of a sign is an eight-sided red STOP sign. It refers to traffic laws and the institutions that enforce those laws. A stop sign means one thing and one thing only. Symbols, on the other hand, refer to something beyond themselves and carry multiple meanings. In addition, symbols draw us into those meanings. Symbols make present in the here and now stories and ideas from other times and places. This is why we show respect for such symbols, especially the central symbols of Christian faith.[10]

Especially in the Lutheran and Episcopal churches included in this book, respect for Christianity's central symbols is clearly seen. At Christ Lutheran Church in Richmond, Virginia, the reading of the Gospel text for the day is always accompanied by a Gospel procession. The people stand as the procession—including the processional cross carried by a crucifer, candles carried by torchbearers, the Gospel book carried by the Gospel bearer, and the priest—comes to stand in the midst of the people. Christ is praised, and people make the sign of the cross, acknowledging the presence of Christ among them in the reading of the Gospel.

Christ Lutheran Church, Richmond, Virginia. Photo by Dave Swager. Used with permission.

At Grace Episcopal Church in Newton Corner, Massachusetts, the baptismal font evokes this respect by its very size. It stands over three feet tall when uncovered, and with the cover in place is at least five feet tall. Its three-part construction evokes the Trinitarian formula of baptism, and the Pascal candle placed next to it is a reminder of baptism into Christ. The font stands near the door that connects the sanctuary with the rest of the church's buildings so most entering worshipers regularly pass the font.

At Christ Lutheran Church in Richmond, the Altar Guild is actively committed to the central symbols, especially the Eucharist. The day before each eucharistic celebration, women gather to prepare the altar table, a process that takes almost two hours. The linen cloths have been washed and carefully pressed. Each liturgical object is polished and set in its appointed place. The worship book is placed for the presider to use and opened to the appointed page. After the celebration the chalice, paten, worship book, and linen cloths are carefully cleaned and put away. Most of this work is done in silence, and the women refer to it as a personally formative spiritual practice.

The respect shown these central symbols is, first of all, respect shown to Jesus Christ. As the Directory for Worship of the Presbyterian Church (U.S.A.) makes clear, Christ is present in the church by the Holy Spirit through these central symbols.

Grace Episcopal Church, Newton Corner, Massachusetts. Photo by author.

Christ Lutheran Church, Richmond, Virginia. Photo by Dave Swager. Used with permission.

Jesus Christ is the living God present in common life. The One who is proclaimed in the witness of faith is

(1) the Word of God spoken at creation,
(2) the Word of God promising and commanding throughout covenant history,
(3) the Word of God
   (a) who became flesh and dwelt among us,
   (b) who was crucified and raised in power,
   (c) who shall return in triumph to judge and reign.

Scripture—the Word written, preaching—the word proclaimed, and the Sacraments—the Word enacted and sealed, bear testimony to Jesus Christ, the living Word. Through Scripture, proclamation, and Sacraments, God in Christ is present by the Holy Spirit acting to transform, empower, and sustain human lives.[11]

God in Christ is present by the power of the Holy Spirit in these symbols, and that presence is acknowledged by symbolic words and actions as the community of faith gathers for worship.

As communities made up of persons who live complex, often-demanding lives, this encounter with the risen Christ can be disorienting and disturbing. The symbolic words and actions of worship serve to call us out of our customary self-preoccupation and invite us to be taken up into the very life of God.[12] And it is obvious to anyone who worships regularly that this transformation is not dependent on the "right" words, the "right" gestures, the "right" liturgical actions. The words, gestures, and actions of the worshiping assembly must be given life, an internal energy that comes from deepening discernment of God's presence being given expression in embodied worship. "Participation in the hidden languages of time and space[,] of sound and sight, of taste, texture, and bodily movements is an essential condition for the human words to become God's living Word to us and for the signs employed to become living symbols."[13]

There is a "profound and mysterious reciprocity between body and spirit,"[14] says Ronald Byars. The gestures and stance of worship leaders communicate the presence of this reciprocity. Here's a negative example that may illustrate a positive point: I was a visitor in a church having a very large sanctuary and a very small baptismal font and pitcher. Nevertheless the associate pastor was taking seriously the guidance from the report on the sacraments adopted by the Presbyterian Church (U.S.A.) *Invitation to Christ*. The report recommends placing the font in the midst of the people and filling it with water each Lord's Day. It further recommends that worship leaders "lead appropriate portions of weekly worship from the font."[15] Often this is done by pouring water into the font during the confession and declaration of pardon. As the report notes, "What we do and how we do it convey meaning every bit as much as what we say."[16] This pastor's body spoke loudly as he poured a little dab of water into the font, being careful to keep his elbow close to his ribs so that, in the end, the gesture was hardly visible to the congregation. His posture, movements, and use of liturgical objects (font, pitcher, water) spoke loudly of his doubt that God could speak through material objects, and especially not in worship.

Steve Shussett, a converted Jew who remembers with longing his upbringing among Jews whose worship always included the body, writes of "embodied spirituality," spirituality that includes the use of the body and all its senses in worship, prayer, and adoration of God, even as it stresses appreciation for God's creation. Shussett quotes John Calvin: "We are cold when it comes to rejoicing in God! Hence, we need to exercise ourselves in it and employ all our senses in it—our feet, our hands, our arms and all the rest—that they all might serve in the worship of God and so magnify him."[17] Shussett says embodied spirituality is primarily a spirituality of doing and being rather than thinking and knowing. He is not suggesting that thinking and knowing should be replaced but that our notions of spirituality should be expanded. He also says that while reflection on practices is necessary, explanations of embodied practices should not overshadow or replace the practices themselves.[18]

When we hear the phrase "the language of the liturgy," most of us think immediately of the words. We think of ideas and concepts written into prayer books and liturgical guides. We would do well to think more broadly of the "languages" of the liturgy, of the gestures, actions, colors, furnishings, and the arrangement of church building itself in combination with the words. These symbolic languages, when taken together, form a rich metaphorical vocabulary that allows worshipers to "see through" the symbols with a kind of depth perception that reveals more truly the reality of God, ourselves, and the world, and calls us to radical participation in the worship of God and in the world.

## Juxtaposition

Our family has always had a picture wall, a place in the house where photographs of grandparents, great-grandparents, weddings, new babies, graduations, and all the rest are displayed. The picture frames sit close to one another, almost touching, in what seems like a gathering of the clan. In such an arrangement, aesthetics are not the primary concern. Rather, storytelling is. For the stories to be told, the relationships to be remembered, it makes a difference that pictures of Granny and Papa are hung next to pictures of baby Dan and Mother and Daddy Vann and Aunt Marguerite. Whenever we have moved, the picture wall has been dismantled and reinstalled in our next home. The arrangement is never exactly the same. Nevertheless, pictures are hung with attention to relationships and the stories they tell. Something similar is going on with the liturgy. To the occasional worshiper or casual observer, it may appear that worship is the same week after week. Upon closer examination, however, one can see that in reality, worship is never the same from one week or season or festival to another. The various languages of the liturgy combine in inexhaustible variation in the unfolding of God's invitation.

Symbolic languages carry what is commonly referred to as a surplus of meaning, and this surplus lies, in part, in the ways the various liturgical languages interact with one another. These symbolic interactions, what Gordon Lathrop calls liturgical "juxtaposition," arrange and rearrange themselves around the central symbols, shedding light on the whole of our liturgical celebrations.

The Sunday meeting of Christians, no matter what the denominational tradition, has focused around certain things: primarily a book, a water pool, bread and wine on a table; and secondarily fire, oil, clothing, a chair, images, musical instruments. These things are not static, but take on meaning in action as they are used, especially as they are intentionally juxtaposed. . . . Start with the simple things, the common human materials, then see how communal meaning occurs as these things are juxtaposed to each other and gathered together with speech about the promise of God. In this way, the assembly and the materials it uses become a rich locus of meaning, casting light on all common life and summed up in the shorthand of such technical words as "baptism" and "eucharist."[19]

Lathrop's advice is worthy of our sustained attention. By starting with the central symbols of Christian faith, by allowing them to articulate in their unique languages the message of God's redemption—a message for which words alone are inadequate—the church by its liturgy gives witness to the world that Christ came to save.

## Worship as Play: An Intentionally Irreverent Metaphor

In all my conversations and reading about the liturgy, it has been striking how often it is the artists who "get it." It is musicians, architects, painters, sculptors, and actors who first of all are hungry for ways to worship God that include more than the language of words. Artists are accustomed to communicating in symbolic, metaphorical languages. Symbols and symbolic languages arise, it has been said, because words alone will not suffice. Artistic metaphors, then, provide one way to understand what is really going on in the liturgy. Daniel Benedict describes spiritual engagement in the liturgy as a "Love's dance" that includes God, ourselves, and the whole of creation. "When we participate in the liturgy, we are caught up in mystery—the mystery of God's loving the world and the Paschal mystery as Love's dance—and . . . our lives are entwined with the life of the triune God."[20] The theological term for this dance is *perichōrēsis,* and the accompanying process of spiritual formation is *divinization.*

> Orthodox theology (Eastern Christianity) calls this mysterious journey *divinization*—being taken up into the life of God, sharing in the life of God. This dynamic movement is also termed *perichoresis*—literally, "moving around" as in dancing. The three-in-one God is a community of love dancing with such mutual reverence for each other that this love spills over and reaches out to indwell us and to sweep us up into the life of God creating, redeeming, and sustaining the beloved. In this dance every person and all of creation is beloved. And God desires to indwell the creation with love until all is finally beloved by all of us.

Here we come to the heart of liturgical prayer: we find ourselves dancing with God![21]

Benedict goes on the say that he thinks of the church's liturgy as "God's
playground, with God inviting us to come out and play."[22]

These playful, artistic images appeal to me. For many years I taught three-
year-olds in a church-supported nursery school, and my research during that
time was in the area of children's play. Anyone who has observed children at
play will recognize the ways they are able to transcend time and space. Give
a child a few simple things—crayons, paper, cast-off clothing, clay, blocks,
dishes, and pans—and soon enough they will inhabit a world of their own. For
them the playroom disappears, and they are fully present in a jungle, a home,
or a seashore. They swim, fight, ride horseback, and jump tall buildings. All of
this is done imaginatively, but for the children it is quite real. (Just try disrupt-
ing such a setting, and you will be told how "real" it is!) Similar transcending
moments are common for adults. Think of a movie, play, novel, or short story
that has thoroughly captivated you, when you have been so taken in by the
story that you willingly "suspend your disbelief." Think of a dance, game of
tennis or basketball, sewing project, or construction project that so completely
held your attention that you forgot where you were and what time it was.

The appeal of embodied, richly symbolic liturgy is much the same. When
we gather each Lord's Day to hear the stories, sing the songs, and pray
together, we are invited by the living God to suspend our disbelief and join
in the divine dance. Since ancient times theologians have observed that we
humans require a variety of entry points into this divine dance. Calvin, for
example, insists that teaching and preaching alone are not adequate for our
"receiving Christ." God, says Calvin, does not disdain our need but willingly
comes to us in visible signs suited for our human capacities to understand.[23]
Ronald Byars echoes these sentiments:

> The truth is that there are inward experiences, dispositions, and relation-
> ships that can only be expressed symbolically—even playfully. . . . It's pos-
> sible that God's provision for us of Word and Sacrament is ideally suited
> to the complex beings that we are. It's possible that we may, in words and
> actions just beyond the horizons of understanding, meet the God who is
> always greater than the capacity of our minds to grasp. It's possible that
> our instinctive craving for ritual is part of our original equipment. Possible
> that God intends the sacramental drama to be a means by which God may
> meet us and touch us.[24]

In the following chapters we will explore the various languages that make
up worship and the ways they are woven together.

Chapter 3

# Gathering God's People

## A Place for Worship

*Everything begins with the assembly. God acts. God gathers a people. God makes a covenant. God creates a community. . . . God lives not in a temple, or on a mountaintop, but in the midst of the people, with the people, in the assembly.*

D. Foy Christopherson[1]

*The task of the modern architect is not to design a building that* looks like a church. *It is to create a building that* works *as a place for liturgy.*

Peter Hammond[2]

$A$ll of worship's symbolic languages both shape and express a congregation's understanding of God, themselves, and the world, but the language one is most likely to encounter first is the language of space. The buildings and rooms in which Christians worship surround and influence all of the other languages. For this reason it makes sense to begin our explorations of worship's symbolic languages with attention to the place for worship.

The early Christians understood the church to be the people, called by God through Jesus Christ, in the power of the Holy Spirit, and referred to their buildings as "the house of the church." (See Romans 16:5.) I like this term because it indicates the physical reality and location of our worship, while making clear that the people and the building in which they gather are not the same. Throughout the Scriptures of the Old and New Testaments, we read accounts of the people's encounters with God in many different places. Places such as the altars of the patriarchs, the tent of meeting during the exodus, the temple in Jerusalem, and local synagogues during exile—all were designed to invite and express God's presence. After Jesus' resurrection the disciples continued to gather in the upper room and on the Mount of Olives, where their experience of the presence of Jesus was vivid. Not surprisingly, many of these locations were remembered as special because of these encounters. Still today when the church gathers, in whatever place, it is the presence of the risen Christ in their midst that forms the center point of worship.

Liturgical space and environment are meant to create a setting for the assembly to worship God. Gilbert Ostdiek calls this a holy climate. "Good liturgical space invites people to experience the presence of the Holy One in their lives and conveys the feeling of wholeness and healing that comes from being God's own."[3] Whatever else worship space may be, it is first and foremost a place of encounter for God and God's people. Robert Hovda describes this encounter in both negative and positive ways, naming what the meeting *is not* as well as what it *is*.

> The assembly. It's not a town meeting, not a neighborhood council, not an elite, not a gathering of cronies, not a party for friends, not a household event, not tribal, not family, not civic, not ideological, not an occasion for manifesting ecclesiastical distinctions, . . . but an overwhelming manifestation and realization-in-action of the unity of the body of Christ, the oneness of the baptized. It is the covenant celebration of mission, of call—collective call and mission of standing for and inching the world toward the freedom and the oneness of all people which we believe are gifts of God.[4]

The house of the church, then, is the place of this "realization-in-action" of the covenant between God and God's people. The only reason for the church to have a "house" is for the embodied enactment of worship. Or to say it another way, the primary symbol for the church is the gathered community at worship. The house of the church serves the congregation as it gathers, anticipating an encounter with God.

As God's people we have no other way to enter into life than in our bodies. We orient ourselves with words that refer to our bodies and our embodied place in the world, words like above/below, before/behind, beside. Our bodies and the space that surrounds them form the setting for all other dimensions of our experience. This means that the size, scale, and sensory qualities of a space take on added importance. When a space seems too small or too large, when the actions of the liturgy are distant, when acoustics make it difficult to hear and follow what is said—then our relationship to, involvement in, and response to the liturgy will be affected. We take in liturgical space and environment through all the senses, including sight, sound, smell, touch. Space and environment can have a certain "feel" depending on the space's size in relation to the human body. We notice the size of the space, the height of the ceilings, whether it is spacious or crowded, well-organized

MATT 18:20
WHENEVER TWO OR MORE ARE
GATHERED IN MY NAME, I AM
THERE AMONG THEM.

Gathering God's People    33

or cluttered, and much more. We notice smells, textures, shapes, light, and dark. The acoustics, natural and artificial light, and dimensions of a worship space can either facilitate or inhibit the worship of the community that gathers there, and these factors influence our participation in the liturgy.

Because liturgy is a shared participatory activity (as opposed to a spectator sport), space serves the liturgy best when it allows for easy participation. The congregation and its leaders need room to move as they participate. On the other hand, the space should be arranged so that it does not swallow up the gathered assembly. The space should serve the worship event that is taking place there and should reflect the community that assembles there. Because worship both shapes and expresses our shared encounter with God and one another, the possibilities and limits of our worship space have a profound effect on us. Yet worship space is often unnoticed and its influence ignored.[5]

The members of ChristChurch Presbyterian in Bellaire, Texas, have spent a lot of time pondering their worship space. The congregation is made up of members from two former congregations whose buildings were about a mile apart. A few years ago it became clear that one strong congregation could carry out Christ's mission more effectively than two struggling ones, and so Bellaire Presbyterian and Braeburn Presbyterian merged to form the new ChristChurch. The buildings of the former Bellaire church became their new home, and the pastors of the two congregations became copastors. Lacy Sellers and Mark Cooper worked closely together to bring the two congregations together in ways that would signal their new beginning. One early project was the redesign of the sanctuary, which now did not suit the needs of the newly formed congregation. The overly large sanctuary with its elevated pulpit and lectern, distant communion table, absent baptismal font, and choir out of sight behind chancel railings—all made the church feel empty and put worship leaders far away from the people. Copastor Mark Cooper argued strongly for change. "The people of Braeburn were already coming onto someone else's turf. They were giving up all of their property. It was important for there to be a radical shift for the Bellaire congregation, too." The Building Renovation Task Force took three months to design the changes to the sanctuary. Then it took two weeks of do-it-yourself work to complete the renovations. The congregation worshiped in the fellowship hall for only one Sunday.

As they planned, the Task Force read about worship space design, including a most helpful chapter in *Beyond the Worship Wars*, by Thomas Long.[6] The chapter on worship space recommends that congregations provide space for gathering; congregation space; choir space; movement space; and pulpit, font, and table space. Long's terms indicate that the action of the gathered congregation governs the arrangement of worship spaces, not architectural

ChristChurch Presbyterian, Bellaire, Texas. Photo by Dan O'Keefe. Used with permission.

design. Thinking of space in this way—in terms of the liturgical action that takes place in that space—leads many to speak of "liturgical centers." Rather than calling attention to specific places like narthex, chancel, baptismal font, communion table, or pulpit—the term "liturgical center" reminds us of the action taking place and that action's meaning.[7]

At ChristChurch Presbyterian, the placement of the pulpit, font, and table now declare their centrality for the life of the congregation. The people surround these central symbols. The chancel railings are gone, and the choir now sits across the platform. A new lower platform holds a pulpit, lectern, and table. The baptismal font, a glass bowl with a bubbling fountain, is at the entrance to the worship space in the center aisle. Pews have been rearranged so that the two front sections on either side of the aisle are set at an angle facing the pulpit and table. This layout has avoided the stage-and-audience arrangement, which signals to the assembly that their role is to be passive while worship leaders carry out worship on their behalf. Instead, the whole congregation is gathered around the pulpit, font, and table, where they embody and participate in the liturgy as a whole people of God. Almost half of the remaining pews from the back of the sanctuary have been removed,

ChristChurch Presbyterian, Bellaire, Texas. Photo by Dan O'Keefe. Used with permission.

creating a spacious gathering space. Dividing the worship and gathering space is a stained-glass room divider. Three of the four panels are replicas of the windows of Braeburn Presbyterian, made by the same stained-glass studio. The fourth panel is the new ChristChurch Presbyterian logo, a multilayered cross set in a colorful sunburst. The process of design and renovation of the worship space was a thoroughly collaborative project. As they redesigned the place in which they worship, the two former congregations became one, giving witness to the new thing that God is doing in Bellaire.

## Who God Is and Who We Are

All of the mainline denominations included in this study share the conviction that worship space both shapes and expresses the church's convictions about what it means to be the body of Christ, the company of the baptized. *Principles for Worship* of the Evangelical Lutheran Church in America (ELCA) begins with affirmations about the formative nature of worship and worship spaces:

Worship forms people for Christian ministry. The space and its visual appointments share in the formation of those called to be Christ's body in the world, proclaiming the word through nonverbal means, teaching the faith through image and symbol, and offering their own witness to the gospel. Christian mission is enlivened by and inseparable from the worship of the assembly.[8]

The United Church of Christ *Book of Worship* expresses a similar conviction, beginning with the permanent nature of architectural structures and their influence on how congregations worship:

Forms of worship change, but buildings yield to change reluctantly and usually only at considerable expense. Church architecture is a sermon in walls, floors, and ceilings. If its form no longer relevantly announces the good news of God's love that is celebrated in Christian worship, it is the responsibility of the people of God, with the assistance of able architects, to reform the space and rearrange or replace the furniture. Where this is not done, buildings erected to be servants of right worship become rulers that prohibit liturgical renewal or barriers to worshipers because of inaccessibility.[9]

By its width, depth, and height and the resulting acoustics; its arrangement; and its use of light—worship space communicates to us something about the nature of God. And given that all of our notions about God are necessarily incomplete, provisional, and complex, attention to worship space and its complexities is justified. One liturgical designer observes that our understandings of God are, not surprisingly, oppositional and that this opposition is reflected in our church buildings:

Deeply rooted in our faith tradition are oppositional understandings of the nature of God, affirming that God is both transcendent and immanent. When we create church buildings, we often seek to affirm one or both of these aspects of God's nature. . . . Design choices related to the scale, volume, light, decor, and organization of the churches we create affect the perception of the God we represent and serve.[10]

When analyzing worship space, it is important to keep in mind both the immanence and transcendence as well as other characteristics of God so that the nonverbal means of communication natural to architecture (and all of the arts, as we shall see in the next chapter) offer glimpses of the gospel in all its fullness and variety.

At Spanish Springs Presbyterian Church in Sparks, Nevada, one might think it impossible to include both these dimensions of God's nature in a worship space carved out of a leased strip-mall space. The boxlike nature of the building itself yields to the creative ways in which leaders of the congregation have arranged their use of it. The hallway leading to the worship space includes several necessary turns that serve to draw worshipers away from the commercial environment and into the worship space itself. The room is arranged on the diagonal, with the primary liturgical center for Word and sacrament located in the far corner. The room features handmade liturgical furnishings and simple folding chairs. The walls are pale in color, and the few visual adornments include a handmade cross and small banners. The typical commercial ceiling of suspended acoustical tiles is slightly vaulted, giving more height in the center and sloping to a standard height at the walls. These simple features serve to draw worshipers in and guide their attention to the encounter with God embodied in the liturgy. As this community gathers for worship, it is difficult to recall that we are in a strip mall. And that is as it should be. The space serves the worship of the people. Its intimate size helps them to discern God's presence among them while at the same time communicating God's grandeur.

The multiple turns of the hallway at Spanish Springs are not merely a function of necessity. The turning of the hallway that leads to worship provides worshipers with space and time to orient themselves toward worship. The layout of the worship spaces of other congregations allows for similar reorientation. At Bethlehem Lutheran Church in Saint Cloud, Minnesota, the long driveway leading from the street to the parking lot was intentionally designed to provide a gradual transition into worship. According to planning committee member Bette Raffenbeul, "People have many frustrations in life and getting ready for church. We planned the site with a 'tranquility drive.' By the time people drive in, they are relaxed and ready to worship." Liturgical architects and building planners say these sorts of entryways are inspired by the mystery and grandeur of God. "Many new worship spaces now have labyrinthine pathways leading to great portals inspired by mythological definition. The interiors are graced by high ceilings, ample natural light, and seating configurations that draw worshipers into the liturgical activity not as spectators but partners in the ritual dance."[11]

At Saint Stephen's Episcopal Church in Richmond, Virginia, there are multiple services in the grand stone church building, where every arch, aisle, and altar declare the transcendent glory of God.

In addition to these services, young children and their parents meet in Palmer Hall Chapel, the original church building, for a weekly "instructed liturgy," where worshipers are "coached" through the liturgy and its meanings are explained as the service goes along. The space is small, with the

Spanish Springs Presbyterian Church, Sparks, Nevada. Photo by Doug Ramseth. Used with permission.

altar/table and the pulpit close to and on the same level as the gathered worshipers. Murals depicting benevolent hovering angels adorn the walls. The intimacy and natural welcome of the space declare God's immanent presence. Betsy Tyson, who coordinates the Palmer Hall worship, says, "Palmer Hall is casual. The sermons and format and instruction are comfortable. It is a huge draw for families returning to the church and for young kids. Once they become part of it, they become like a small community. There are lots of dads in their mid-20s and 30s." Children take the lead in all parts of the service, acting as acolytes, torchbearers, chalice bearers, readers of Scripture, and choir. Children are learning as they go, says Betsy. "Parents are *hungry* for faith; they want things that focus on faith and daily life."

## Memory and Hope

We worship a God of the past, present, and future. Given this truth, our worship spaces should facilitate our remembrance of God's mighty deeds

Saint Stephen's Episcopal Church, Richmond, Virginia. Photo by Sarah Bartenstein. Used with permission.

Saint Stephen's Episcopal Church, Richmond, Virginia. Photo by Sara Bartenstein. Used with permission.

throughout history and vividly anticipate the future promised in the life, death, and resurrection of Jesus Christ. All of this we celebrate in the present every time we gather for worship. By its very nature, worship space is a place of memory, where life cycles are celebrated in baptismal, confirmation, marriage, ordination, and funeral rites. More important, stories of faith throughout history are repeated and reflected upon in ways that serve to include present-day worshipers in those stories. The stories of faith become *our* story. Further, worship spaces inspire the human imagination to envision what might be. These twin agents of transformation—memory and imagination—serve to move worshipers beyond the boundaries of the present and draw them into the formative past and the transformative future. According to Richard Vosco, worship spaces are extensions of religious experience, settings that place us at the intersection of past, present, and future so that we come to know the God of our forebears and to follow God's leading into the future.

Worship spaces can be resonators when the stories of the faith community are apparent in the very design of the building. The use of color, light, scale, and art, as well as the incorporation of pathways, portals, and centers can contribute to the religious experience. The worship space is a story-book of old tales and many chapters still unwritten.[12]

Worship space does more than tell us who God is and draw us into God's presence. All of Christian worship also looks toward the fulfillment of God's saving intentions for the whole creation. Christian worship anticipates and participates in that ultimate future by remembering God's promises and remembering who we are as redeemed people before God. Don Saliers reminds us that

> at the heart of all Christian prayer and worship is the cry for God's will and covenant promises in Jesus Christ to be made real. . . . So the [Lord's Prayer] asks that God's reign be found growing in our actual life, that we receive and flourish in the promises of God, and that the final triumph of God's justice and righteousness be expected. This is a way of translating, "Seek first the kingdom of God."[13]

Worship space also tells us who we are before God, a people of hope and expectation. Gilbert Ostdiek says,

> Liturgical environment . . . tells us that we are a people, a people summoned by God's word, nourished by the grain of wheat that fell into the ground, and sent to invite a world into a kingdom. It tells the story of our journey as disciples, how we met the Lord Jesus on the way and were sent to tell the others. Its manner of telling is not that of audible words which chronicle beliefs and deeds, but rather that of the subtle voices known only to the other senses, voices which lead us to feel in our bones what it means to be God's people. We decorate and shape the environment of our gathering place to embody that message in full sensory fashion, and the environment in turn shapes us.[14]

## A Place of Encounter

Worship space is for the people and their liturgy. God has promised to be present "where two or three are gathered," and this promise takes on physical form in worship spaces designed to facilitate this encounter between God and God's people. Worship spaces that communicate this central purpose share a number of attributes. First of all, they are marked by the inherent *hospitality* of their design. Hospitable worship space brings people close to one another so they can hear, see, and participate in their shared worship. The space encourages and facilitates the people's involvement. It also anticipates and prepares to welcome people with varying abilities and needs. Issues of accessibility and full participation are at the forefront of liturgical hospitality. Hospitable space provides for the special ministries of musicians and others who provide leadership.

One pastor I know keeps a sign on his office wall that says, "The main thing is to keep the main thing the main thing." If this is true for pastoral ministry, it is certainly true for the church's liturgical spaces. Earlier we have spoken about "liturgical centers" and the need for those places of focused liturgical action and participation to be *clearly defined*. The design and layout of worship space should make clear the centrality of Scripture and preaching, baptism, and the Eucharist and their relationships to one another. Recently the worship leaders and artists at Grace Episcopal Church in Newton Corner, Massachusetts, highlighted their already-beautiful baptismal space with a festive canopy. Constructed of shimmering fabrics in white and gold, the triangular canopy hangs above the large font, catching the light and reflecting it into their baptismal celebrations. Because their font is located in a transept, an alcove adjacent to the chancel, the canopy attracts the attention of worshipers and makes clear its inclusion in the worship of the assembly, whether or not a baptism is being celebrated.

Liturgical space should be *flexible*, allowing for the varying needs of celebrations around the liturgical year. There are recurring shifts in emphasis and focus during the liturgical seasons, and flexible space allows for creativity and full participation. Many congregations have removed some of the pews from their worship spaces to make their worship spaces more flexible. Others have removed pews altogether and replaced them with movable chairs. With increased emphasis on liturgical participation and action, this move toward flexibility is a welcome adaptation.

At Little River United Church of Christ in Annandale, Virginia, the World Communion celebration each fall has become an annual highlight of their liturgical life. The large communion table is moved from the chancel platform to the center of the sanctuary. The movable chairs are arranged in rows all around the table. On other occasions when the choir, which sits on risers at the back of the sanctuary, presents a major musical work, the chairs are turned to face them. Flexibility such as this allows for ease of movement and creative adaptation for a variety of liturgical celebrations. As we shall see in the chapter on the enactment of worship (chap. 5), flexibility of space is an essential component when we are seeking to invite the embodied, active participation of the whole assembly.

Recall for a moment an occasion when some beautiful sight has stopped you in your tracks. Maybe it was a sunset, landscape, or mountain vista.

Grace Episcopal Church, Newton Corner, Massachusetts. Photo by Carol Robinson. Used with permission.

Grace Episcopal Church, Newton Corner, Massachusetts. Photo by Carol Robinson. Used with permission.

Grace Episcopal Church, Newton Corner, Massachusetts. Photo by Carol Robinson. Used with permission.

Maybe it was a painting, sculpture, or building. Beauty can be a "portal to the mystery of God and a witness to Christian faith and truth," according to the Lutheran Principles for Worship.[15] The beauty of worship space begins with the honest use of materials that reveal their natural beauty and point toward the Creator. Attention to design, proportion, and construction allows natural beauty to reveal itself. Beauty in worship space, however, is not an end in itself. It always points beyond itself and inspires encounter between God and God's people. As we have seen at Spanish Springs Presbyterian, careful arrangement and simplicity can create beauty, even in a shopping mall. "Good liturgical space invites people to experience the presence of the Holy One in their lives and conveys the feeling of wholeness and healing that comes from being God's own. It is above all the simple, cared-for beauty of the assembly place that bears for us this sense of the holy."[16]

By the very fact of its existence, worship space declares the message and mission of the church. Worship space is designed to tell the story of God's faithfulness, to declare the good news in Jesus Christ. Worship space

Little River United Church of Christ, Annandale, Virginia. Photo by Mark Holm. Used with permission.

does this by all of its means—by its *hospitality*, its *clearly defined* litur-gical centers, its *flexibility*, and its *beauty*. As they provide the place of encounter, all of these aspects of worship space work together to declare the gospel. The mode of communication is indirect, implicit in the spaces themselves, which makes their construction and use of great importance. Foy Christopherson says, "Spaces, sacred or secular, form people for good or ill. They are catechetical but not didactic. That means they form us, our faith, and our understandings of God and the church by 'whispering in our ear' more than by teaching logically arranged information and content to master."[17]

Attention to worship space and what is communicated by its shape, size, acoustics, lighting, and arrangement is a good way to begin conversations about worship. We can see, touch, and move around in these spaces, making it easier to explore and describe the ways they "speak" as one of the liturgical languages. The questions below are intended to help congregations engage in such conversations, with the hope that worship space may become more and more a place of encounter.

## Ideals and Questions for Discussion

*Choose two or three questions that are important for your congregation.*

1. *Ideal:* Places for worship "invite and express God's presence."[18]
   *Describe* the features of your worship space that indicate God's presence and those that draw attention away from encounter with God.
   *Explain how* these features enhance or inhibit the assembly's awareness of God's presence.
   *Imagine* possible revisions or adaptations to the worship space that might serve the people's encounter with God.

2. *Ideal:* Worship space is a place of memory for the assembly and recalls stories of encounter with God.
   *Describe* the features of the worship space that draw on the people's memory of encounters with God.
   *Explain how* these features evoke memories.
   *Imagine* possible ways the worship space might more strongly evoke the people's memory.

3. *Ideal:* Worship space is a place of hope, where the assembly is called to envision God's redemption and intentions for the world.
   *Describe* the features of the worship space that call the assembly into God's intended future.
   *Explain how* these features communicate hope.
   *Imagine* ways the worship space might more clearly show this eschatological hope.

4. *Ideal:* "A hospitable worship space generously accommodates the assembly, its liturgy, and a broad range of activities appropriate to the life of the congregation and its surrounding community."[19]
   *Describe* the ways your worship space is hospitable. Does it provide a gathering place, a place for the assembly, space for the liturgy, and a place for musicians?
   *Explain how* these spaces support or inhibit the assembly's full, conscious, active participation in the liturgy.
   *Imagine* possible modifications to the worship space that would invite fuller participation.

5. *Ideal:* "The presence of God is celebrated in well-defined spaces for baptism, eucharist, and proclamation. The assembly's focus is supported when all elements of the arts and architecture work as a whole to draw attention to the central signs of word and sacrament."[20]
   *Describe* what the worship space indicates is central. Is it Scripture, preaching, baptism, and/or Eucharist? Is it something else? What?

*Explain how* the worship space shows what is central. What part do place-ment, lighting, and color play? What other attributes help show what is central?

*Imagine* possible adjustments or modifications that would show that Scripture, preaching, baptism, and the Eucharist are central to the church's life.

6. *Ideal:* "Flexibility of space and portability of furniture facilitate the variations of worship as well as related activities of congregation and community."[21]

*Describe* flexible features of the worship space. Describe features that are not flexible. Is the furniture portable?

*Explain what* makes the furniture portable or not.

*Imagine* ways to make the space more flexible and the furniture more portable. What possibilities does this offer for fuller participation in the liturgy?

7. *Ideal:* The beauty of worship spaces is not an end in itself. Beauty in worship "is liturgical, and its purpose is to engage the congregation in the work of worship."[22]

*Describe* what is beautiful and what is not so beautiful in your worship space.

*What makes* it beautiful or not so beautiful? How does it help to engage the congregation in worship? How does it inhibit worship?

*Imagine* ways to enhance the beauty of the worship space in ways that draw us to God and through which God can be known and glorified.

Chapter 4

# Dressing the Space

## Making the Unseen Visible through the Arts

*As Christ takes our flesh with all its flaws and through Spirit-inspired artistry transfigures it, turning it back to us to the glory of the Father, so we are enabled to work within creation as artists. Our art on this model can be truly physical and yet it can be more—it too in a sense can be transformed into an image of grace.*

*William Dyrness*[1]

*O*n Maundy Thursday and Good Friday in many churches, the worship space is stripped of all decoration. Candles, tablecloths, paraments, and even the cross are removed or covered. Look at a worship space during these days of Holy Week, and it will become apparent how significant the visual arts are as a language of worship. We know the church's seasons and their moods by the way the worship space is "dressed" (to use a theatrical term). The contribution of the visual arts to the other languages of worship is to make plain the nature of the church's celebrations as the arena for encounter with God. In this chapter we will examine some ways the language of the arts communicate the liturgy's intentions and imagine ways this language creates worship's overall environment.

Several years ago our family vacationed in Italy. Part of our itinerary took us to the ancient city of Ravenna, where we visited churches in which Christians have worshiped since the fifth century. Entering these ancient buildings, one is immediately struck by their beauty. Mosaics are on almost every wall. We saw beautifully carved baptismal fonts, altars, and pulpits. The churches had alabaster windows and gracefully adorned archways. Artisans of every kind—sculptors, painters, metalworkers, mosaic artists, and more—gave their best and most creative efforts both to honor God and to draw worshipers into God's presence. These ancient worship sites and most worship sites throughout history demonstrate that art and worship are natural companions.

In today's congregations the arts enhance the environment for worship and include furnishings, banners, paintings, sculpture, stained glass, vestments, chalice, paten, candlesticks and candles, processional crosses and torches, flower arrangements and vases, offering plates and baskets, and much more.

There is a strong case to be made for greater attention to and appreciation for the arts as formative in the Christian life. The relationship between the arts and Christian worship calls for sustained care because, without it, a haphazard and possibly *deformative* environment may emerge. As we noted in the previous chapter, the qualities of our surroundings influence our way of seeing God, the world, and ourselves.[2] According to historian Robin Jensen,

> The architecture of the church building, the stained-glass windows, the organ music, and the flower arrangements may be taken for granted instead of evaluated or challenged. But surely they have an impact on how we think about, image, and worship God. And if we begin to pay that kind of attention to how all these things together inform and affect our faith, we might begin to wonder how we could have gone so long without noticing. And once we start to notice, we cannot help but be critical as well as appreciative. We may want to make changes.[3]

Most of us are accustomed to "understanding" through spoken and written words. We like to have things explained in step-by-step understandable ways. But in reality our ideas are made up of images, the things we see, hear, smell, taste, and touch. Long before we know words to say what we know, we experience and begin to make sense of the world through our senses. We may communicate these ideas in words, but their image quality is always close at hand. As we gather to worship, the images and objects that surround us call for careful attention because, whether we are aware of it or not, they influence the ways we think and understand. At various times in the church's history the arts have been employed faithfully, used improperly, and rejected altogether. When the church has gone so far as to reject imagery in worship, it is a stance that does not belittle images but acknowledges their power. No matter how carefully they are chosen, images bring with them subtle yet powerful feelings and convictions.[4] Today there is increasing awareness of the indispensible place of the arts in worship as well as emerging criteria for their faithfully formative inclusion.

We learn from Augustine that beauty and our attraction to it is "evidence of divine grace, irresistible, magnetic, and salvific; it [is] God-initiated, not human-willed. The power of our recognition stems from the fact that we are created in the image of God, and so share in a marred but original beauty."[5] Our human attraction to beauty is not for our pleasure only. Both natural and artistic beauty call us to a deeper level of relationship to that which is beautiful and to the creator of that beauty.[6] Such an understanding of the arts, especially the arts in worship, requires great care as we seek to include the arts in worship.

We have said all along that worship is centered around the Christian community's encounter with God. The place of the arts in worship is to foster and enhance that encounter. James and Susan White write that it is the function of art in the liturgy to "make visible the unseen presence of God":

> Part of the purpose of liturgical art in the church is to underline the seriousness of what we are about when we gather for worship. This is not a casual assembly; this is the people of God meeting with God. . . . The value we place on worship is emphasized by the quality of the environment we provide. . . . The chief function of [liturgical art] is to make visible the unseen presence of God, although the image can never be confused with that which it depicts. It is art that commands us to take off our shoes as we recognize that the ground on which we stand is holy, that we are in the presence of God. No ordinary art will do this. We do not produce a photographic likeness of God, but a representation that points beyond itself to what the inner eye alone can see. Thus there is a transcendent quality to art. It has power to make present to our minds the transcendent One, just as photographs of loved ones can help to mediate their presence when absent. But unlike the loved one, God is present; we simply need to be reminded of this reality, and liturgical art helps to do this.[7]

The act of giving careful attention to an object, particularly an object of beauty, produces in us a response, a reaction. The reaction may be positive or negative, evoking rejection, attraction, excitement, disappointment, or grief. The change may be slight or profound. Whatever our response, we are changed by the encounter. It is not the onetime act of attention, however, that is ultimately transformative (although there are occasions where this is the case). Rather, it is sustained attention over time on which Christian spiritual formation depends. In recent years there has been a renewed emphasis on Christian practices and the need for sustained engagement in them. Similarly, our engagement with the beauty of worship and its environment could be seen as an element of Christian practice. It is in seeing again and again those material objects that "make visible the unseen presence of God" that Christian spiritual formation can take place.

It is natural to speak of the arts and spiritual formation with individual persons in mind, but as we know, at its heart Christian worship is a communal gathering. Or as one teenager I know said, "Christian faith is not an 'I' thing. It's a 'we' thing." Thus the environment for worship shapes the whole community. Many years ago I attended a meeting of the regional governing body of my denomination at a rural church. This particular congregation had a reputation in the region for being particularly discouraged and quarrelsome. As I entered the worship space, the room in which the meeting was to take place, I was shocked by the visual image that confronted me. A very large stained-glass window dominated the space. It featured a somewhat familiar image of Jesus praying in the garden on the night before his death, but instead of the typical stone at which he is usually shown to kneel, the figure of Jesus was draped across a huge rough-hewn stone cross. Rather than the good news of the gospel, this congregation lived under the perpetual shadow of the tragedy of the cross. For this congregation it was never Easter. I wondered how the image in their stained-glass window formed the character of the congregation. Works of art that help to form the environment for worship are not only the expression of an artist or the preference of a church arts committee. Rather, the environment for worship "exists for the whole community and should speak to them as well as expand their vision."[8] We will deal more specifically with the process of evaluation and selection of art for the liturgical environment later in this chapter. For now it is well to recognize the formative qualities within the worship environment and to recall Gilbert Ostdiek's understanding of worship preparation as "caring for God's people at prayer."[9]

At Bethlehem Lutheran Church in Saint Cloud, where the worship space is grand in scale, the inclusion of the arts in worship has made a significant contribution to the worship life of the congregation. Season by season the artistic expressions that fill the space convey the themes of the season and week by week are modified and enhanced to mark the progression of the season.

In chapter 2 we reviewed the distinction between signs and symbols, making the point that symbols carry with them a depth of meaning, built up over time through repeated encounter, that gives them an intimate relationship with the thing signified. Because we are embodied creatures and cannot exist otherwise, we depend on our senses in order to engage the world. Objects and images that have form and substance are the means by which our minds depend in order to understand realities beyond the material world.[10]

The arts give expression to our understandings of God, the world, and ourselves and draw us into God's presence. We need to be cautious here, however. Though symbols present the nonmaterial, they ultimately fail to disclose it completely and are never to be mistaken for the thing signified. The result would be idolatry. Ongoing critical reflection on symbols is necessary and can contribute to the congregation's spiritual formation.[11]

Bethlehem Lutheran Church, Saint Cloud, Minnesota. Advent. Photo by Larry Grover. Used with permission.

It almost goes without saying that in many congregations this kind of critical reflection—conversations about and instruction concerning the liturgy for children, youth, and adults—has been missing for far too long. This is *not* the case at Saint Luke's Lutheran Church in Park Ridge, Illinois. In this thriving congregation of more than a thousand members, all aspects of the congregation's life are organized around full participation in and understanding of the liturgy by everyone.

Their sanctuary is filled with beautiful artwork including stained-glass windows and murals depicting biblical stories, images of women saints, and fabric art highlighting the liturgical seasons, crafted by the congregation's artists. Some of the congregation's most skilled musical leaders are children and youth. (More about the musical arts in chapter 8.) In all of these artistic endeavors, the congregation's educational leaders take an active part in helping the members engage with, understand, and reflect on the meanings of their symbols. Educators Dee Weinke and Paula Besler help to prepare children and youth for worship by teaching about the symbols in the sanctuary.

Bethlehem Lutheran Church, Saint Cloud, Minnesota. Christmas. Photo by Larry Grover. Used with permission.

Bethlehem Lutheran Church, Saint Cloud, Minnesota. Lent. Photo by Larry Grover. Used with permission.

Confirmation students have worksheets of worship notes that ask them to reflect on the theme and symbols of each worship service. There are e-mail communications each week that help children connect the stories learned in Sunday school with the texts for the week's liturgy and the music learned in choir. All these ways (and more) ensure that the necessary interpretation of worship's symbols is a natural part of this congregation's culture.

Even a hasty assessment of contemporary culture would show the rise and prevalence of visual images as a form of communication. In the case of the liturgy this may be a very good thing. Often I have been present in services of worship that were rich with artistic symbols and liturgical action, only to observe those around me staring fixedly at their worship programs, seemingly afraid to miss a single word. When I give students an assignment that asks them to plan worship, many of them turn in a worship program, assuming that this provides everything one needs to know about a particular worship event. William Dyrness urges that we avoid unnecessary competition between the visual and the verbal when seeking to make room for the visual arts:

> Christians should not play the visual against the verbal. . . . [There are] biblical grounds for affirming the visual as theologically significant. God

Bethlehem Lutheran Church, Saint Cloud, Minnesota. Easter. Photo by author. Used witb permission.

Bethlehem Lutheran Church, Saint Cloud, Minnesota. Ordinary Time. Photo by Larry Grover. Used with permission.

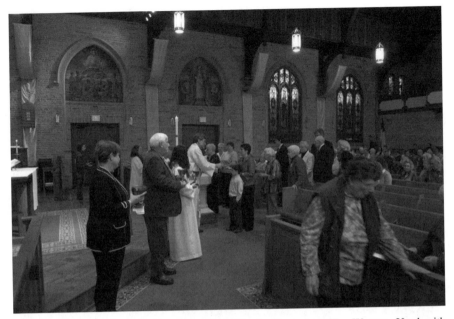

Saint Luke's Lutheran Church, Park Ridge, Illinois. Photo by Mike Watson. Used with permission.

> lovingly fashioned a creation that sparkles with signals of [God's] tran-
> scendence, and [God] in fact entered into the creature's depths in Christ
> and began there the process of transformation from within. The temple, the
> visions of the prophets, the spectacle of Pentecost, and the vision on Pat-
> mos all serve as precedents to encourage Christians to exercise a sanctified
> visual imagination. They even give us warrant to claim the stimulus of the
> Holy Spirit for the project.[12]

Dyrness admonishes Christians to "recover their visual imagination" for the sake of a new visual literacy and the possibility of fresh imaginative insight.[13]

Worship has always been multisensory and multimedia. It involves sight, sound, movement, smell, taste, touch, and more. Thus Don Saliers argues:

> The physical senses are crucial to the recovery of awe, delight, truthful-
> ness, and hope. For worship depends upon our capabilities of sensing pres-
> ence, of hearing, seeing, touching, moving, smelling, and tasting . . . simply
> because Christian worship is physically, socially, and culturally embod-
> ied. . . . And knowledge of God is never purely intellectual.[14]

Theologians agree that visual imagination and sacramental imagination are integrally related, enabling us "to imagine God as present in the world and the world as revelatory instead of bleak."[15] And as emphasized in chapter 2, human imagination is one means of revelation used by God to initiate the human/divine encounter.

## Technology, Media, and Liturgical Arts

The use of electronic technology has been seen as a natural extension of older media as well as a means to better communication of the gospel. In recent decades many congregations have sought to embrace the relationship between visual images and spiritual formation through the use of visual media technology. They seek to stimulate visual and sacramental imagination, enhance communication, and go beyond print and spoken words to proclaim the gospel and the mission of the church.[16] Visual media provide greater liturgical access, especially to those with disabilities. But the use of visual media technologies in worship also brings with it a set of perils that must not be ignored. These include the influence their use has on worshipers' level of participation.

The use of screens to project musical lyrics, for example, does get worshipers' heads up and away from texts printed on paper, but it is not always clear that their participation is increased. It may be that their visual attention is simply shifted to the screen. The hoped-for shift from spectator to participant in the liturgy is not always achieved. The use of visual media in the form of video clips or projected visual images may result in worship becoming entertainment. If the goal is to attract greater attendance, there is the temptation to allow entertainment values to dominate and to downplay the substance of the gospel. Some critics argue that the use of visual media in this way contaminates worship with the values of popular culture. In some congregations the acquisition and use of the most up-to-date technological hardware and software has been labeled by some as idolatry, as concern for media production values comes to overshadow the central intentions of worship itself. All of these possibilities and perils call for careful research, reflection, and experimentation when expanding the use of media technologies in worship.

Only one of the congregations described in this book made regular use of media technology (other than sound amplification) in worship. When they renovated their sanctuary, ChristChurch Presbyterian in Bellaire, Texas, hoped to include a projection screen but delayed its introduction until other changes were comfortably in place. Careful thought and planning went into decisions about the size and placement of the screen as well as the kind of equipment needed, given the high level of ambient light in the room. They made sure that the screen could be removed when not in use for a particular event.

ChristChurch Presbyterian, Bellaire, Texas. Photo by Dan O'Keefe. Used with permission.

## Faithful Use of the Arts in Worship

In setting criteria for the use of visual media technology in worship, Eileen Crowley proposes three measures that are relevant to all of the arts. Crowley says that visual media should be judged as to whether or not they are *"appropriate, fitting,* and *integral* to the community's ritual actions, interactions, and liturgical arts, and worship space."[17] But how do congregations come to know what is appropriate, fitting, and integral to the community's worship? The process of discerning and articulating criteria for liturgical arts comes from reflecting on the nature of the liturgy itself, its theological intentions, and on past practice. The process also depends on careful observation and reflection on the ways particular communities enact their worship and are formed by it.

All of the denominations represented in this book have entered into this kind of study, reflection, and discernment, and they have produced documents for the guidance of congregations and their worship leaders. In a

ChristChurch Presbyterian, Bellaire, Texas. Photo by Dan O'Keefe. Used with permission.

paragraph titled "Artistic Expressions" the Presbyterian Directory for Worship says:

> The Reformed heritage has called upon people to bring to worship material offerings which in their simplicity of form and function direct attention to what God has done and to the claim that God makes upon human life. The people of God have responded through creative expressions in architecture, furnishings, appointments, vestments, music, drama, language, and movement. When these artistic creations awaken us to God's presence, they are appropriate for worship. When they call attention to themselves, or are present for their beauty as an end in itself, they are idolatrous. Artistic expressions should evoke, edify, enhance, and expand worshipers' consciousness of the reality and grace of God.[18]

The Evangelical Lutheran Principles for Worship goes further, stating that "when an art form participates in the liturgical action, it becomes an instrument of proclamation rather than decoration or ornamentation. Liturgical art reinforces and articulates the themes of the liturgy."[19] The United Church of Christ *Book of Worship* affirms that the liturgical arts "summon worshipers to unite with their neighbors on the pilgrimage toward" the future that God has redeemed and promised.[20] Artistic expression is fitting when its presence in worship fulfills these aims, the aims of worship itself.

Artistic expressions are appropriate when they attend carefully to the specific liturgy being enacted. Again, the Evangelical Lutheran *Principles for Worship* notes that planning for the celebration of the liturgy begins with the study of the liturgical texts and readings appointed for the season and the day.[21] We will say more about the liturgical year in chapter 6. It is enough to say here that the setting for worship should reflect the liturgical season, and the arts are a necessary component of the seasonal environment. A congregation's anticipation of participation in the story of God's redemption can be significantly heightened through the use of the visual arts season by season.

As we noted in chapter 2, at Tustin Presbyterian Church in Tustin, California, the church has given careful attention to several of the arts in order to shape the seasonal liturgical environment. Artistic and symbolic creativ-

Tustin Presbyterian Church, Tustin, California. Photo by Helen Anderson. Used with permission.

Tustin Presbyterian Church, Tustin, California. Photo by author.

ity informs the designs of the new pulpit, lectern, font, and table. The pulpit features a Trinitarian trefoil design and has seasonally changeable panels. The font and table are octagonal, a shape that points to Christ's resurrection as the "eighth day of creation, the first day of the new creation." The table features hand-carved images of wheat and grapes. Sue Currie prepares the sanctuary for worship each week and says, "I am the Altar Guild." She often meditates on the symbolic imagery in the sanctuary's artistic appointments: "Having the font and table and pulpit together is part of the Reformed faith. That's Calvin. It is not just about aesthetics that things should match. You want them to go together because they *belong* together." Over the course of several years the church has commissioned a full set of seasonal paraments and tablecloths. In addition, there are banners and floral wall decorations for each season. The quality and care of these artistic expressions are evident and reflect the congregation's understanding of the capacity of the arts to call the congregation into God's presence.

Artistic expressions are part of the enacted, participatory worship of the people and provide a rich multisensory environment in which the liturgy takes place. As we have seen, the arts can contribute to the people's

Tustin Presbyterian Church, Tustin, California. Photo by Helen Anderson. Used with permission.

discernment of and attentiveness to the presence of God in their midst. But as the United Church of Christ *Book of Worship* notes, "The arts are not immune to abuse. Frequently the church has had to deal with the issue of artistic forms that obscure the gospel rather than proclaim it."[22] We have all seen art that obscures the gospel. In addition to art that calls attention to itself and is for decorative purposes only, issues of good design, quality materials, careful construction, size, scale, and proper placement are necessary considerations.[23] When the arts serve the liturgy, the whole environment for worship functions as a harmonious whole to support and enhance the assembly's active participation.

The use of technological media is subject to all of these theological and aesthetic criteria and more. The timing, pace, rhythm, and choreography of media with all other elements of liturgical action contribute to the whole of worship. This includes where and how media is displayed; the position, size, and scale of screens in relation to the space; and their level of dominance in relation to other visual elements. It is also important to consider how much time will be devoted to projected images and for what purposes. Attention should be given to the aesthetic dimensions of projected images themselves. Like all art in worship, projected images should reflect artistic sensibilities that take into consideration contrast, alignment, color relationships, and repetition. When using video, consideration must be given to motion, rhythm, tempo, timing, repetition, flow, and the balance between sound and silence. Eileen Crowley observes that "A sense for aesthetics can make the difference between a photo or graphic that communicates and one that irritates."[24]

## Liturgical Arts and Congregational Decision Making

Anyone who has spent time in the church is probably well aware of the complex and often treacherous dynamics of congregational decision making. It should come as no surprise that these dynamics are likely to be fully in play when considering the arts and worship. With this in mind, it bears repeating that the arts are intended to serve the liturgy and to be integral to the assembly's active participation in the worship of God in a particular context. Any group seeking to reflect on and provide works of art for worship should share agreement on this point and should spend time exploring and clarifying its demands in their particular setting. The process of more fully including the arts in worship is a process of discernment and should be approached prayerfully and in an unhurried, deliberate manner. Openness to honest give-and-take discussions, to learning something new, and to the guidance of the Holy Spirit is essential. An arts-and-liturgy group should include pastors, congregational leaders, and those with particular skill, interest, expertise, and experience with liturgical arts. In addition, the group should be committed to recruiting others to help create and evaluate the arts in worship, especially those who are wary of such a project. I make it a point to admonish students never to be Lone Rangers in ministry: the planning, preparation, and evaluation of the liturgy are areas of church life where this is especially important. With practices of discernment in place, an arts group can proceed with visits to congregations where the arts are well established; with brainstorming, congregational education, times of experimentation, congregation-wide feedback; and with reflection on what has been learned. Crowley calls this sort of process "communal co-creation." Writing about media ministry, but equally applicable to arts ministries in general, she says, "Instead of a closed circle, liturgical media ministry has permeable boundaries. By design it would have many openings through which people could enter the process as they were interested and able."[25] After a long period of separation (and maybe mutual disdain) between the church and the arts, the church seems poised to invite professional artists into its liturgical life and begin a process of mutually fruitful collaboration.[26]

Foy Christopherson suggests three levels of evaluation that help organize the many complex decisions confronting arts ministry groups. Levels of evaluation include theological evaluation, pastoral evaluation, and aesthetic evaluation. Theological evaluation is the natural starting point and includes consulting Scripture, denominational documents, and the practices of the congregation's particular tradition. Second are pastoral concerns, evaluated in terms of the *pastoral* intentions for worship (often articulated in denominational documents), concern for those with disabilities, and the ongoing practices of the congregation. Third, aesthetic evaluation would include assessment of a work of art's design, construction, materials, color, size, proportions, and liturgical use.

> *Theological evaluation* (primary)
> If it passes—
> > *Pastoral evaluation* (secondary)
> > If it passes—
> > > *Aesthetic evaluation* (tertiary)
> > > If it passes—
> > > > *Implementation*[27]

The process of welcoming the arts into the liturgical life of the church may seem complex and even daunting, but its possible rewards are many. As to the obstacles, it may just be that in working through such difficulties, congregations will learn new ways of living together in Christ. Frank Burch Brown offers this bit of advice: "It is an act of Christian love to learn to appreciate or at least respect what others value in a particular style or work that they cherish in worship or in the rest of life. That is different, however, from personally liking every form of commendable art, which is impossible and unnecessary."[28] Our efforts to include the arts more fully in worship may or may not have liturgical artistic results, but they may school us in other Christian virtues and call us to deeper levels of mutual understanding.

The language of the arts gives expression to the church's celebration in ways that words cannot; it moves worshipers to a deeper level of engagement. For this reason the use of the arts in worship requires great care and consideration. As we have seen, the arts can distort as easily as they can enhance our worship. The more worshipers and their leaders become attuned to the symbolic language of the arts in worship, the more the use of the arts can be employed to open worshipers to the presence of God. Let the arts speak their word, to the glory of God.

## Ideals and Questions for Discussion

*Choose two or three questions that are important for your congregation.*

1. *Ideal:* Liturgical arts are intended to make the unseen visible and awaken worshipers to God's presence. In this way they are integral to the liturgy. When the arts call attention to themselves, distract, obscure, or serve only as decoration in worship, they fail in their purpose to proclaim the gospel.

   *Describe* your congregation's use of the arts in worship.

   *Explain how* particular works of art make the unseen visible, awaken worshipers to the presence of God, and proclaim the gospel. Explain how particular works of art distract, obscure, or distort worshipers' awareness of God's presence.

   *Imagine* possible changes to the artistic environment for worship that might draw worshipers into God's presence.

2. *Ideal:* Liturgical arts "summon worshipers to unite with their neighbors on the pilgrimage toward" the future God has redeemed and promised.[29]

   *Describe* the artistic elements of your congregation's worship that unite worshipers with their neighbors.

   *Explain how* these artistic elements serve to unite worshipers. Explain how artistic elements divide or exclude some neighbors.

*Imagine* further artistic inclusions that might broaden and deepen the shared life of the assembly.

3. *Ideal:* The arts call worshipers into regular and sustained contemplation of beauty as reflected in creation and the material world. This contemplation has ethical implications, motivating worshipers to become more beautiful and more good.

*Describe* works of art that call worshipers to ethical action.

*Explain how* worshipers are motivated toward ethical commitments and actions.

*Imagine* possible changes in the environment for worship that might lead to ethical commitments and actions.

4. *Ideal:* Liturgical arts "enrich the assembly's participation in the word and sacraments."[30]

*Describe* your congregation's use of the arts in relation to Word and sacraments.

*Explain how* these practices enrich the assembly's participation. Explain how these practices might inhibit the assembly's participation.

*Imagine* revisions in the congregation's use of the arts that might better invite their participation in Word and sacraments.

5. *Ideal:* The liturgical arts are to be suited to each particular celebration and "reinforce the themes of the occasion and season."[31]

*Describe* the use of the arts to reinforce the themes of particular celebrations. Describe uses of the arts that inhibit the realization of the themes of particular occasions and seasons.

*Explain how* the arts reinforce or inhibit the clarity with which the themes of the seasons are realized.

*Imagine* possible changes in the use of the arts that might reinforce the themes of particular occasions and seasons.

6. *Ideal:* The liturgical arts are fittingly adapted to each congregation's unique social, cultural, and historical context.

*Describe* elements of the liturgical environment that express the unique context of the congregation. Describe elements of the liturgical environment that falsely express the congregation's context.

*Explain how* these elements are truly expressive or falsely expressive of the context.

*Imagine* possible changes in the liturgical environment that would be more truly expressive of the congregation's context.

7. *Ideal:* Artistic elements used in worship should be of good design and careful construction and be made of quality materials. Their size, scale, and placement are meant to support the liturgical celebration of the assembly.

*Describe* the aesthetic qualities of the liturgical environment of your congregation.

*Explain how* these aesthetic qualities enhance or detract from the assembly's worship.

*Imagine* possible changes in the liturgical environment that would enable the liturgy to better fulfill its theological and pastoral intentions.

8. *Ideal:* Effective use of media technology in the liturgy depends on appropriate placement of the technological hardware and the effective timing, pace, rhythm, and choreography of its use.

*Describe* your congregation's use of media technology in worship.

*Explain how* this technology supports and enables the assembly's worship of God. Explain how the technology inhibits or detracts from this primary purpose of the liturgy.

*Imagine* possible modification in the congregation's use of technology in the liturgy.

Chapter 5

# Enacting Worship

## Using Our Bodies in Worship

*The body, as a temple of the Spirit, is a primordial sacrament of Christ's presence. Through gestures and postures, worshipers extol their Creator with their whole being. They approach that perfect uniting of the outer and the inner that awaits us in a new heaven and earth.*
Craig Douglas Erickson[1]

*In* introductory speech classes it used to be a common practice to restrain a speaker's hands and arms in order to demonstrate how much we humans depend on bodily movement and gesture in order to communicate. In the church the movement and gesture we use is sometimes spontaneous and at other times expected and customary. In either case, the use of the body goes beyond our spoken words, to enlarge our vocabulary of praise, lament, confession, and worship of God. In this chapter we will examine the symbolic vocabulary of movements and gestures and the ways they contribute to worship.

My family is always giving me coffee-table books, and they usually feature eye-catching photographs and floor-plan diagrams of beautiful church buildings. Some of these books feature historic churches built long ago and far away. Others survey contemporary church architecture. Still others feature worship spaces from across the world's religious traditions. What is striking about these books is that the photographs seldom have people in them. They rarely show a congregation gathered in God's name. To my eye these worship spaces without people in them seem incomplete, unfinished.[2] No matter how large or small, grand or humble, beautiful or not, worship space is incomplete and somewhat meaningless without the gathering and participation of worshipers. To say it another way, worship is a verb.[3] Sacraments are verbs.[4] Worship is something we do with our whole bodies, not just our voices, with our spirits as well as our minds. Worship is a "doing"

71

with words. We shall have more to say in the next chapter about the relation-ships between the actions and proclamations of worship, but for now we want to concentrate on that aspect of worship that has sometimes been neglected or even rejected in Christian worship: the embodied gestures and actions that make up worship.

The actions and gestures of worship are both functional and symbolic. They include simple things such as movement from one part of the worship space to another and also the profoundly symbolic communication of such things as carrying a processional cross and signing the cross on the forehead of a worshiper. As such these actions and gestures are the "body language" of the church.[5] The Principles for Worship of the Evangelical Lutheran Church in America says it this way:

> Actions in worship, such as gesture, ritual movement, dance, as well as the visual and architectural environment, are significant elements of wor-ship. Sometimes these nonverbal elements communicate powerfully on their own, and sometimes they support and enhance the words that they accompany.[6]

The actions of worship—gestures of welcome, prayer postures, signs of blessing, the kiss of peace, the preparation of worship space, and liturgical processions—are complex actions (accompanied by words) that participate in the central mystery of faith to which they point. Liturgical actions and gestures communicate and make present the reality of God's self-giving. Especially in the sacraments—where bodies are bathed in abundant water, bread is broken, wine poured out, and all are fed—we see clearly the signs of blessing and know of God's nearness and care.

Congregations of the Evangelical Lutheran Church in America recently adopted the *Evangelical Lutheran Worship* hymnal and service book (2006), replacing the 1978 *Lutheran Book of Worship*. Like many Evangeli-cal Lutheran congregations, the people at Christ Lutheran Church in Rich-mond, Virginia, spent many months preparing to receive the new book. The almost-thirty-year tenure of the previous service book meant that many in the congregation had experience with no other worship patterns and had great affection for the "green book." Leaders of the congregation knew that the changes called for by the new "berry book" would need time before they were incorporated into the congregation's life and formation. Never-theless, they were eager for the enriched worship promised in the new book. Over the course of many months they used advance copies of new musical settings and, with the choir's leadership, tried out some new ways of wor-shiping. They told stories of the ways their faith had been formed by the hymns, prayers, and settings in the green book. At the end of the service, on the last Sunday of its use, worshipers were asked to carry their hymnal out of the sanctuary and either take it home or leave it on one of the tables in the church's gathering space. Parishioners looked through the stacks of green hymnals, searching for bookplates showing that a particular book was given in honor of a loved one. Almost everyone left with a book under an arm.

The next Sunday the hymnal racks in the pews were empty, but a table stacked with the new berry books greeted the people as they came into the gathering space.

As Pastor Eric Moehring, the crucifer, torchbearers, choir, and worshipers formed the procession, each worshiper carried a new book into worship. This congregation, so accustomed to embodied liturgy, naturally marked the farewell to one service book and the reception of another through the physical act

Christ Lutheran Church, Richmond, Virginia. Photo by author. Used with permission.

of carrying the old books out of the worship space and the new ones into it. They said with their bodies what was in their hearts.

But not all congregations and denominational traditions are so fortunate, and many long for more-embodied worship. My former colleague Ronald Byars describes inviting a metropolitan of the Russian Orthodox Church to visit his church for evening prayer. "As he entered the chapel, he approached the Communion table: slowly and with remarkable grace, he bowed deeply from the waist. I was jealous. . . . I was jealous of one who came from a community that did not feel uncomfortable showing respect for material objects that symbolically represent Christ's presence in the midst of the worshiping assembly. . . . I was jealous as well of the metropolitan's freedom to worship with his body as well as with his mind."[7] Byars goes on to explore what he calls the "profound and mysterious reciprocity between body and spirit."

Scripture offers many opportunities to explore this profound mystery, beginning with the creation of the world and the place of humans within it. In the creation stories of Genesis, after chaos is ordered and the material world is created, God declares the world to be good. It is within this declaration of goodness that the use of our bodies in worship is to be understood. Kathryn Sparks puts it this way:

> It is uncharacteristic of the Old Testament to subdivide the human being. In Genesis 2, God stoops down and picks up the dust of the earth, fashions it, and breathes into it; and this becomes a living being (Genesis 2:7), a living soul. "He [the human] does not *have* a soul. He *is* a living soul. . . . He does not possess his flesh. He *is* flesh." Both the Old and New Testaments assume that the human being is a unity of matter and spirit. "There are no Hebrew equivalents for 'body' and 'soul' since it was understood that only the living, embodied male or female existed."[8]

Each human being, then, is an embodied being whose very existence points toward the Creator. Sparks says that each one of us is "an embodied prayer from the heart of God." The division between body and soul, inner contemplation and outer expression, is better understood as a kind of reciprocity, community, and mutuality rather than a competitive hierarchy. In chapter 2 we spoke about the communal "dance" or "play" within the life of the Trinity, a communal celebration of being in which we too participate, body and soul. Each of us as a living soul participates in this embodied "dance" of the spirit.

One of the central affirmations of Christian faith, along with the goodness of creation, is the redemption of creation through embodiment in the incarnation of Jesus Christ. "In the incarnation God becomes human, becomes embodied, for our redemption. In the incarnation God enters our fragmentation, becoming broken for us so that we might be restored to unity and harmony."[9] God makes use of the created world, including human bodies, to make present the new creation toward which worship and especially the sacraments point. By the power of the Holy Spirit, the church becomes the "body of Christ" in the world, called to share Christ's love and justice in every place. The final portion of the Great Prayer of Thanksgiving says it this way:

Gracious God,
pour out your Holy Spirit upon us
and upon these your gifts of bread and wine,
that the bread we break
and the cup we bless
may be the communion of the body and blood of Christ.
By your Spirit make us one with Christ,
that we may be one with all who share this feast,
united in ministry in every place.
As this bread is Christ's body for us,
send us out to be the body of Christ in the world.[10]

These and other scriptural and theological warrants point worshiping communities toward worship that invites our full-bodied and full-hearted response to the living God.

At Saint Stephen's Episcopal Church, the Sunday evening Celtic Evensong is filled with liturgical action. This contemplative service features meditative music and a church filled with candlelight.

Leaders for this service—musicians, lectors, pastors—arrive an hour early to make sure all is in order. They enter the church and take their places at least fifteen minutes before the service begins. As worshipers gather, there is a mood of silent attentiveness already present. Pastors Gary Jones and Weezie Blanchard say, "We want to establish the ambience into which people will enter." This service includes silent and spoken prayers, during which members of the congregation are invited to come forward to light a candle as an act of prayer.

Later in the service, people come forward for communion, eating and drinking together as the body of Christ. Many worshipers choose to meet a minister in one of the side chapels for healing prayer. There, with arms around the shoulders of each one, ministers pray with and for the concerns of those who seek. Prayer and caring embodied in this way speak more loudly than words.

We have described embodied spirituality as primarily a spirituality of doing and being rather than thinking and knowing. This is not to suggest that

Saint Stephen's Episcopal Church, Richmond, Virginia. Photo by Sarah Bartenstein. Used with permission.

Saint Stephen's Episcopal Church, Richmond, Virginia. Photo by Sarah Bartenstein. Used with permission.

thinking and knowing should be replaced but that our notions of spirituality should be expanded. Embodied spiritual practices are a kind of "muscle memory." Through embodied practice our capacity to come before God as whole persons is strengthened and deepened. We should be slow to say, "Been there, done that"; instead, we should slow down and explore the embodied practices common to Christian faith and let them inform our thinking and knowing.[11] At the same time it is wise to find an appropriate balance between "muscle memory" and rote ritualism.

Embodied worship has at least two purposes. One purpose is communication. Through the use of *sign-acts*—the symbolic combination of action and words in the liturgy—the Christian assembly makes clear to itself and in witness to the world who and what is central to Christian faith. In fact, the very words we say in the liturgy depend in large measure for their meaning on the bodily actions that they accompany. Don Saliers claims that "ritual actions such as blessing, anointing, washing, giving and receiving the kiss of peace, and others mentioned in the New Testament combine saying and doing into potent signs of grace."[12] These sign-acts announce repentance, reconciliation, forgiveness, and hope by embodying their reality in both word and gesture. As such, the words require human action and touch. But the church insists that these sign-acts communicate more than human meaning. Christian sign-acts, especially the sacraments, communicate God's grace. Made up of rich combinations of embodied human gestures, material objects, and words, sign-acts become complex symbols that not only signal God's presence and activity but also participate in that divine presence. Further, they serve to draw human participants into the very life of God. "Thus the human actions designated by the Christian tradition, derived from God's fullness in Jesus Christ, point beyond themselves and take part in the divine reality imparted to those who receive."[13]

The second purpose for the sign-acts of Christian liturgy is derived from the first. As we are drawn into the divine life of the Trinity, we are changed. We are redeemed, reconciled, strengthened in faith, commissioned. Through the mysterious reciprocity of body and spirit, we are spiritually formed for the fullness of the community's praise of God and for the mission of the church in the world. Many communities speak of the "journey inward and the journey outward," indicating the inseparability of Christian formation in the image of Christ and the compassionate engagement of Christians in the world. When worship reflects this reciprocity, the relationship between worship and mission is clearly communicated.

## Worship's Sign-Act Vocabulary

The primary sign-acts of Christian worship are the reading of a story, a bath, and a meal. In the act of reading Scripture, the making of new Christians through baptism, and eating bread and drinking wine together, the church shows forth Christ. We in the Presbyterian Church (U.S.A.) are learning this anew as we live out the recommendations of the church's report on the sacraments, *Invitation to Christ: A Guide to Sacramental Practices*.[14] I was privileged to be a part of the study group that prepared this report. We spent three years praying together, studying Scripture, studying the history of the church and its liturgy, and worshiping together. In good Presbyterian fashion the study group anticipated preparing an academic report along with a set of recommendations concerning the "rules" for the celebration of the sacraments. In the end, however, in a moment of Spirit-led inspiration, we recommended a set of sacramental *practices*, actual physical activities in which the church is invited to participate. We recommended that congregations

1. Set the font in full view of the congregation;
2. Open the font and fill it with water on every Lord's Day;

3. Set cup and plate on the Lord's table on every Lord's Day;
4. Lead appropriate parts of weekly worship from the font and from the table; [and]
5. Increase the number of Sundays on which the Lord's Supper is celebrated.

Further suggestions accompany each practice and invite congregations to experiment with them to find patterns of sacramental practice that are appropriate for them. Water in the font reminds us of our baptismal identity. In baptism we are washed clean and claimed as Christ's own. Whenever the church baptizes a new Christian, every Christian is renewed in life-giving water. At the Lord's Table we are united with the risen Christ and fed so that we might become the body of Christ in the world. The presence of the cup and plate makes us hungry for this heavenly food and calls us to enact our union with Christ more frequently.

When *Invitation to Christ* was adopted, congregations were invited to share the stories of their experiments with others through a Web site sponsored by the Office of Theology and Worship. As I hear from congregations all across the church, it seems that these sacramental practices are being enthusiastically embraced. Through these central acts of the church—baptism and Eucharist—congregations are learning with their bodies what it means to be the community of the baptized.

Gestures and sign-acts in worship come to us as a rich inheritance from Scripture and the Christian tradition, and as natural human responses to the Divine. It is not just the sacraments that can be understood as sign-acts. From beginning to end, the entire liturgy is a series of sign-acts. Worship begins with signs of *hospitality and welcome*. I doubt that Woody Allen was speaking of the liturgy, but his words nonetheless are apt: "Ninety percent of life is just showing up." The first thing we do in worship is show up, show by our physical presence that we are part of God's people assembled for no other reason than to worship. As living temples of the Holy Spirit gathered as the body of Christ, we show Christ's presence by our own presence. "The presence of Christ in worship is actualized by individual Christians being physically present to each other."[15] This presence is signaled in our smiles, eye contact, handshakes, embraces, and loving attention mutually bestowed. It is also communicated through preparation for worship by both leaders and members of the assembly.

At Bethlehem Lutheran in Saint Cloud, the confirmation class was brought face-to-face with the importance of liturgical hospitality. The pastors were intentionally "naughty," says Pastor Dee Pederson. "In confirmation we spent four weeks on worship, or 'anti-worship.' We did things in an unprepared, casual, lackadaisical way. Well, the students were *upset!*" They knew that poorly prepared, inhospitable worship is not just rude. It is also deeply flawed and possibly fails as true worship.

The church has always practiced a rich variety of *postures for prayer.* One of the most ancient postures, featured in several catacomb paintings, is the standing posture for prayer. Christians are shown standing erect, with arms outstretched and eyes lifted. In the ancient world and still today, to stand in someone's presence is understood as an act of respect. In Jesus' own Jewish tradition, standing was the customary posture for prayer. For Christians, this prayer posture indicates reverence for God and also the freedom and dignity bestowed in the new covenant. In ancient times kneeling for prayer (and fasting) on Sundays, the day of Christ's resurrection, was considered unlawful. In addition to expressing confidence in God's merciful redemption, when Christians stand for prayer they express anticipation for Christ's return. St. Basil the Great writes,

> We stand for prayer on the day of the resurrection to remind ourselves of the graces we have been given: not only because we have been raised with Christ and are obliged to seek the things that are above, but also because Sunday seems to be an image of the age to come.[16]

The Lutheran and Episcopal churches featured in this book all practice standing for prayer, as recommended in their denominations' official worship materials. With guidance from the ancient church and the robust spiritual formation found at these churches, other denominations may see the wisdom of embodied worship practices, including standing for prayer.

Some of the more evangelical and free-church traditions practice *raising the hands* for prayer. This practice, too, has roots in the ancient church. Lifting the hands—arms open, palms up—seems to be a natural gesture for prayer. This *orans* (praying) gesture indicates a plea for God's presence and help. It can also demonstrate an offering of oneself to God. When the hands are lifted, the heart is also lifted. Today we see those presiding at the Eucharist employ this gesture; perhaps with inspiration from both contemporary and historical sources, it will be recovered for the whole church.

Along with the *orans* position for prayer comes the lifting of the eyes. Raising the eyes communicates and embodies an attitude of praise and blessing to God. There are several accounts of Jesus' lifting his eyes in prayer, at the raising of Lazarus, for example. For those of us taught at an early age to bow our heads and close our eyes for prayer, it may be surprising to learn that many of the church's prayers are eyes-open prayers. The Prayer of Great Thanksgiving at the Eucharist is especially notable as an eyes-open prayer, which makes sense given the liturgical actions of taking bread, blessing it, breaking it, and giving it for all to eat. Without the visual participation of the assembly, this sign-act makes no sense. As the design of many of our church buildings suggests, the architects assumed that the people would be looking up. With eyes open and raised, participating visually in liturgical action, our awareness of the presence of God can be heightened.

Kneeling for prayer also shares in an ancient biblical tradition. The early church fathers came to view kneeling as a posture of penitence, and its use was encouraged during seasons of fasting such as Lent. Likewise, as we have seen, its use was discouraged during Eastertide, the season of celebration and joy at the resurrection. While kneeling for prayer is always to be considered a natural posture for Christian prayer, its use might be reconsidered, alongside other possible postures. Sitting as a prayer posture has a relatively short history, and its use is not found in biblical and early-church sources. It emerged after the Reformation, when pastoral prayers gradually increased in length and Protestant congregations grew tired of standing for these "mini-sermons of exhausting length."[17] In terms of liturgical spiritual formation, congregations might want to consider the effects of standing for prayer as the early church fathers recommend. Craig Erickson recommends theological and pastoral criteria for evaluating the use of prayer postures: "The relative effectiveness of all prayer postures ought to be evaluated theologically and pastorally. From the perspective of psychological integration, standing with uplifted hands is preferable to merely standing, and kneeling [is] better than sitting."[18]

Christian communities throughout history have given embodied expression to acts of *blessing*, especially with the hands. The touch of human hands often has a soothing effect and naturally conveys blessing and divine grace. All acts of the laying on of hands have their roots in baptism, where in the ancient church anointing with oil and the laying on of hands accompanied prayers for the gift of the Holy Spirit. Rites of ordination and reconciliation reflect their baptismal roots in the laying on of hands. Especially in times of crisis and illness, hands are placed directly on individuals as prayers of blessing are offered. The raised hands of the presider, often while sending the congregation out, indicate a similar act of blessing. There are congregations where rigid social formality makes touching as an act of blessing rare. In these congregations, where the laying on of hands might bring dread, a reluctant fingertip on the shoulder might convey a message other than blessing. Robust, confident, sincere gestures convey their intended blessing. Shy or unwilling touch does not.

Making the *sign of the cross* is a treasured gesture in many Christian traditions, yet almost unknown in others. During times of past religious controversy, some branches of the church discouraged its practice because it was used by their adversaries. They seemed to be saying, "If *they* use the sign of the cross, *we* won't." The sign of the cross is the mark of God's own name, a sign of God's ownership and protection, and an act of personal dedication. Used throughout worship, the meaning of the sign of the cross is indicated by the liturgical context. At the reading of the Gospel, worshipers use their fingertips to sign themselves with the cross of Christ on the forehead, lips, and chest. Presiders often make the sign of the cross over the waters of baptism and over the bread and wine of the Eucharist. Anointing with oil at baptism is done with the sign of the cross. After eating and drinking at the Eucharist, worshipers often sign themselves with the cross by touching the forehead, chest, and each shoulder. "The touch of God leaves an indelible imprint upon the human soul. The spiritual marking of the Christian is accomplished by the Holy Spirit. It is natural and befitting that this inward and invisible grace should be expressed through an outward and visible sign."[19]

The recovery of *sharing a sign of peace* in worship has been controversial in many congregations where there has been reluctance to interact with other worshipers. This practice, like many of the other gestures of Christian worship, has ancient roots with scriptural and historical references. Although in some congregations it has become a friendly greeting, it has a much deeper spiritual meaning. In offering the peace of Christ to one another, Christians recognize the presence of Christ in one another and offer peace, forgiveness, and reconciliation that only Christ can guarantee through the power of the Holy Spirit. "The Peace is a spiritual encounter. Each Christian is a vehicle of God's grace, and thus a primordial sacrament. When the Peace is exchanged, persons become means of grace to each other. Warmth, genuineness, and spontaneity best convey that peace which passes all understanding."[20] The sign-act of exchanging the peace of Christ may occur at the beginning of the service as a response to God's forgiveness, after the prayers of the people, or immediately before the Eucharist. Wherever it is placed in the service, it should convey the congregation's intention to greet one another in the power of the Spirit.

Actions of *preparing the space for worship* include all of the preparatory actions for baptism, the Eucharist, as well as for seasonal events such as "the hanging of the greens" at Advent, the stripping of the altar during Holy Week, and the dressing of the altar on Easter. When the appearance of the worship space is changed to match the season, worshipers are drawn more deeply into the story of God's redemption. Sunday by Sunday, congregations anticipate meeting Christ in the Eucharist as they observe and participate in the preparation of the table. The gifts are brought forward with other offerings, and bread and wine are set out for the celebration. When water is poured into the font at baptism and wine is poured at the Eucharist, we are reminded of God's love poured out for us in Christ. During the Eucharist the sign-acts of taking bread, breaking it, blessing it, and giving it to all are powerful invitations to discern the presence of Christ.

At Christ Lutheran Church the stripping of the altar on Good Friday and redressing it on Easter morning have been long-standing traditions and have been formative for the congregation. Piece by piece, all of the candles, the Bible and bookstand, the chalice, the paten, the tablecloths, banners, and paraments are removed from the sanctuary. Members of the altar guild come up the side aisle one by one and receive an item from the pastor, then exit by the center aisle. A single voice sings, and the room gradually becomes darker and darker. When everything is removed, all leave in silence. This somber mood contrasts starkly with the mood of celebration on Easter Sunday. When the congregation enters, there are only Easter flowers in sanctuary. One by one, altar guild members bring in the tablecloths, paraments, candles, Bible, chalice, and paten. The room is brightly lighted, and there is music from a brass ensemble. Altar guild members Linda Pickles and Judy Garnett say, "Now, that's Easter!" "Observing the worship space change in color, texture, and intensity at the hands of other members of the congregation can offer some of the most moving dimensions of sign-acts," says Don Saliers.[21]

Christ Lutheran Church, Richmond, Virginia. Photo by Dave Swager. Used with permission.

Lutheran and Episcopal sisters and brothers well understand the formative effects of liturgical *processions*. Processions have both practical and symbolic importance in worship, helping to move groups of people from one place to another in an organized manner and, at the same time, giving bodily expression to the importance of what is being done. As we noted in chapter 3, there are "liturgical centers" where the central actions of Christian worship take place. Processions enable appropriate liturgical action to take place in these various centers and also heighten the importance of the action itself. This chapter began with a description of an entrance procession. Gospel processions carry Scripture into the midst of the standing congregation so that the presence of Christ in Scripture might be proclaimed. Processions that bring the people's gathered offerings into the center of the worship space declare the assembly's intention to "give our very selves to God." At Christ Lutheran, offerings of food for a local food pantry are gathered by the children in a wagon procession in the center aisle of the church.

Processions to the font for baptism, processions of brides and grooms at weddings, processions of the dead for burial—all proclaim entry into the covenant of grace and its sustaining presence throughout our lives "unto eternal life." Processions out of the church and into the world are sign-acts demonstrating that the church is "sent to follow the Word into the world."[22]

Christ Lutheran Church, Richmond, Virginia. Photo by Dave Swager. Used with permission.

Many congregations have found their worship enlivened and renewed through the practice of *sacred dance*. It was common in both Jewish and early Christian worship, but its use was critiqued and discontinued under the influence of theological trends that emphasized denial of the body. Like all of Christian worship, the intention of sacred dance is to honor God. Thus sacred dance, like all forms of music in worship, is not be understood as a performance but is to be regarded as a series of embodied gestures that serve to draw worshipers into God's presence. "Sacred dance has as its purpose the deepening and focusing of the worship event; it is not merely ornamental or decorative."[23] The gift of sacred dance is the body's ability to give expression to all of the moods and emotion common to human life and present in worship. Liturgical dancer and teacher Rosalie Branigan says:

> Liturgical dance requires the dancer to bare his or her soul in worship. There are no words to hide behind, rarely a character to portray, no literal use of facial expression or gesture—only the abstract essence of a basic idea, text, or piece of music. The body does not lie; therefore, raw, real emotions, shapes, and feelings must be wrung from the depths of the soul in each dance in worship for the dance to be the powerful conduit to God that it is capable of being. Unless this occurs, dance in worship becomes, at best, a technical exercise or, at worst, a mechanical performance.[24]

Sacred dancers exercise discernment and judgment to ensure that their offerings in worship are appropriate to the season, to the particular worship event, and to the congregation and its heritage.

By now it should be obvious that liturgical actions and gestures can carry multiple meanings and can be employed in multiple ways in carrying out Christian worship. Understood in this way, we say that symbolic gestures (as well as other symbols) are *multivalent*. They try to convey what cannot be fully spoken, enacted, or explained—the redemptive self-giving of the creator of heaven and earth. Thus we find the use of action and gesture in our worship a necessary component of giving fulsome praise and glory to God. Nevertheless, it is wise to keep pastoral and theological criteria in mind as we explore the possibilities and make decisions as to how worship will be embodied.

Each congregation will have its own wisdom and judgment about the use of movement and gesture, based on the history and heritage, size, resources, and ethos of the congregation, with the aim always to honor God "with heart and hands and voices." The body language of the church offers a rich symbolic vocabulary that can communicate when words are not enough. And in worship, words are *never* enough.

## Ideals and Questions for Discussion

*Choose two or three questions that are important for your congregation.*

1. *Ideal:* As the body language of Christian worship, liturgical actions are both functional actions and symbolic gestures that draw out the meaning of the liturgy itself.

   *Describe* some of the most common actions of your congregation.

   *Explain how* these actions function in practical and/or symbolic ways.

   *Imagine* possible changes in the congregation's embodied "vocabulary." What gestures might be suggested to the congregation? What might their symbolic meanings be?

2. *Ideal:* "In baptism, the Holy Spirit binds the church in covenant to its Creator and Lord. The water of baptism symbolizes the waters of creation, of the flood, and of the exodus from Egypt. Thus, the water of baptism links us to the goodness of God's creation and to the grace of God's covenants with Noah and Israel."[25] "In Baptism, we participate in Jesus' death and resurrection. In Baptism, we die to what separates us from God and are raised to newness of life in Christ."[26]

   *Describe* the baptismal practices of your congregation. Where does baptism take place? Who is involved? What do they do and say?

   *Explain how* these practices embody the meaning of baptism. Explain how the waters of creation, the flood, the exodus, and Jesus' baptism are shown through sound, sight, touch, use, and quantity of water. Explain how the practices of baptism show Christ's death and resurrection. Explain how these sign-acts fail to show the fullness of baptism.

   *Imagine* ways the baptismal practices of the congregation might be changed so that they more clearly show the fullness of baptism.

3. *Ideal:* "The Lord's Supper is the sign and seal of eating and drinking in communion with the crucified and risen Lord."[27] "The New Testament describes the meal as a participation in Christ and with one another in the expectation of the Kingdom and as a foretaste of the messianic banquet."[28]

   *Describe* your congregation's practices of the Lord's Supper. How often does the assembly celebrate? What gestures do presiders and other leaders use? What gestures does the assembly use? How is the Eucharist served? What other liturgical actions accompany the celebration?

   *Explain how* these actions and gestures show the Eucharist to be "the sign and seal of eating and drinking in communion with the crucified and risen Lord."[29] Explain how liturgical action or its absence diminishes the assembly's discernment of Christ's presence.

   *Imagine* ways of celebrating the Eucharist that might make its meanings more apparent to the assembly.

4. *Ideal:* A congregation's repeated actions and gestures provide a kind of "muscle memory" for worship.

*Describe* the actions and gestures that are engrained in your congregation's way of worshiping.

*Explain how* these actions and gestures support and deepen worship. Explain how they might become "rote" and lose their meaning. How would you know if this were happening?

*Imagine* ways to regularly enrich the congregation's "muscle memory" through intentional reflection on these practices.

5. *Ideal:* Through the use of "sign-acts," the Christian assembly makes clear to itself and in witness to the world who and what is central to Christian faith.

*Describe* the sign-acts that are central to the life of your congregation.

*Explain how* these sign-acts witness to what is central to Christian faith. Explain how these sign-acts might obscure or misdirect attention from what is central.

*Imagine* possible revisions to the congregation's sign-acts that would make the central claims of faith more clear.

6. *Ideal:* Gestures of welcome and hospitality celebrate the promises and grace of God.

*Describe* the ways your congregation extends hospitality to friends and strangers.

*Explain how* these gestures celebrate the promises and grace of God. Explain how they might obscure Christ's welcome.

*Imagine* possible changes in the congregation's practices of hospitality so that Christ's welcome is clear and inviting.

7. *Ideal:* Prayer postures show reverence and honor to God and demonstrate the reality of Christ's redemption in the life of the Christian.

*Describe* the typical prayer postures of the congregation.

*Explain how* they show respect and honor for God. Explain how they demonstrate the reality of Christ's redemption. Explain how the congregation's prayer postures might obscure these meanings.

*Imagine* possible changes in the prayer postures of the congregation. How might the congregation's view of God and of themselves be changed by the use of revised prayer postures?

8. *Ideal:* The act of blessing by laying on of hands or raising of the hands conveys Christ's blessing. Sharing the peace of Christ acknowledges the presence of the spirit of Christ in every Christian.

*Describe* the gestures of blessing most often used by the congregation. Describe the occasions for their use.

*Explain how* these gestures convey blessing and acknowledge Christ's presence in every Christian. Explain the possible ways the gestures fail to convey blessing or convey some other message.

*Imagine* possible changes in the congregation's practices of blessing. Imagine conversations that might help revise the congregation's ideas about social politeness, sincere touch, and God's blessing through human hands.

9. *Ideal:* The sign of the cross reflects the mark of God's ownership and the presence of Christ in persons and through the use of objects in worship such as the Bible, water, bread, and wine.

   *Describe* your congregation's use of the sign of the cross.

   *Explain how* it communicates God's ownership and Christ's presence.

   *Imagine* possible uses of the sign of the cross by worship leaders and members of the congregation. What relationship might its use have to "body memory" and spiritual formation?

10. *Ideal:* Preparing the space for worship as an integral part of worship draws the assembly more deeply into the story of God's redemption.

    *Describe* the occasions on which the space for worship is prepared.

    *Explain how* this preparation draws the assembly more deeply into the story of the day or the season. If such preparation is not part of the congregation's tradition, explain how the story might be diminished.

    *Imagine* ways the congregation might incorporate preparation of the worship space into its liturgical life.

11. *Ideal:* Processions help to move people to liturgical centers. They also symbolically indicate to the assembly the importance of these liturgical centers in the assembly's liturgical life.

    *Describe* the ways processions are used in your congregation and their practical usefulness. Describe their symbolic importance for the assembly.

    *Explain how* processions communicate their symbolic meanings.

    *Imagine* new or revised uses of processions and their possible symbolic meanings for the assembly.

12. *Ideal:* Sacred dance honors God and is meant to deepen and focus the worship event.

    *Describe* the congregation's experience with sacred dance.

    *Explain how* sacred dance has honored God and deepened and focused a particular worship event.

    *Imagine* possible occasions for sacred dance in your congregation.

Chapter 6

# Timekeeping

## Liturgical Days and Seasons

*Christians are called to assume a cruciform posture: Standing
upright with feet firmly planted in the present, we stretch out one
arm to grasp our heritage and the other arm to lay hold of our hope;
standing thus, we assume the shape of our central symbol of faith:
the cross. If either hand releases its grip, spiritual disaster threatens
as the sign of the cross becomes misformed. . . . The liturgical observance of past events somehow brings them into our own time.*
*Lawrence Hull Stookey*[1]

*O*ne of the most notable aspects of the church's unique internal culture is
its way of marking time. Nobody keeps time the way the church keeps time.
Rather than the clock and the twelve-month calendar, the church keeps time
with prayers at the rising and setting of the sun, by the priority of the Lord's
Day, and by seasons and festivals that celebrate the events of God's redemption. The church keeps time by remembering the world to God in prayer each
day, by participating in celebrations that recall God's redemptive acts in Jesus
Christ—celebrations that revel in the presence of the risen Christ through the
Holy Spirit's power—and by hopefully anticipating God's final redemption
of the world with the coming again of the risen One. The church's calendar,
shaped as it is by the stories of God's redemption, is a vibrant source for
shaping the assembly's worship and deserves our sustained attention as we
move from Lord's Day to Lord's Day, season to season.

Some years ago a woman who had been raised in the Russian Orthodox
Church joined our small Presbyterian church. As we observed Lent and prepared for Easter, she continued to ask me questions about what to expect.
What did we do? Did we not practice this or that aspect of the season as she
remembered it from her childhood? It didn't take long before I was asking
her questions and learning a lot about Orthodox seasonal liturgical practices.

89

At the end of one of these conversations, she said, "I remember it *being* Easter, not just attending an Easter service. I remember the preparation, the waiting, the anticipation, the absence of certain activities and foods. And most of all I remember the wholehearted celebrations when Easter arrived, when all the light and color and music and festive foods suddenly reappeared. We *lived* Easter!" Immediately I was jealous, both as a Christian and as a Christian educator. Her community was able to engage in the practices and rites of Lent in ways that drew the community into the resurrection life, to which all Christians are called. Here's how a Presbyterian resource states it: "We do not perform Christmas liturgies that duplicate past events; rather, we rejoice in the present reality of Christmas. The festive liturgies throughout the liturgical calendar are not reenacted historical dramas of the past but contemporary encounters with Christ."[2]

My friend encountered Christ through the rites and celebrations of the church. Admittedly, one of the reasons her community was able to achieve this was because hers was an immigrant community, held together by language, customs, family ties, and religion in ways typical North American congregations are not. Her church knew itself to be countercultural, living according to norms and practices that set it apart from others around them. The present-day church can learn from examples like this one. As secularism, consumerism, and the influence of media-driven popular culture increasingly dominate the culture, the church becomes more and more countercultural, living according to norms and practices that are not widely shared.

The seasons and festivals of the church year give the life of the church and the lives of all Christians their natural cruciform shape, as Lawrence Stookey has described it in the quotation at the beginning of this chapter. Cycles of celebration certainly help to form all human communities. Along with most people, Christians celebrate marriages, births, comings-of-age, graduations, and much more, and these celebrations mark events that shape our identities and give meaning to our lives. These events are in turn remembered and celebrated again and again as birthdays, anniversaries, and other repeated festivities. As we go through our lives day-to-day, the overall meaning of our lives is largely implicit. When we pause to celebrate milestone events, we naturally reflect on the meaning of our lives as a whole. In a sense these kinds of celebrations are "outside of time." Celebrations naturally call to mind past events that have shaped us, draw us deeply into present events, and anticipate the future with hope. In this way these repeated celebrations allow us to make our life's meaning explicit. And because they are repeated events, the powerful shaping influence of these milestone events is perpetuated.

In a similar yet more profound way, the church's yearly round of festivals serves to sharpen our awareness of the primordial shaping events surrounding God's mighty acts of redemption and to regularly reflect on their meaning. Like our own personal and family celebrations, the church's festivals exist simultaneously in past, present, and future. According to Stookey, "To be deeply Christian is to know and to live out the conviction that the whole human family dwells continuously at the intersection of time and eternity."[3] He goes on to say that a superficial understanding of Christianity may assume that only certain people [believers] or certain times [Lord's Day worship, certain festivals] dwell at this intersection.[4] Rather, Stookey says, our celebrations—our observance of seasons, days, and hours—should shape the reality of time for all Christians and "make evident the eternal in our midst."[5]

We often perceive time to be linear, to be made up of past-present-future in that never-varying sequence. The church understands time differently. In the church's daily, weekly, and seasonal celebrations, as the stories of God's redemption are told and retold, God's time breaks into our time, and those stories become our story. As we tell and retell the stories of God's redemption, we are drawn by the power of the Holy Spirit into the mystery of Christ's saving work. The annual round of celebrations that make up the liturgical calendar help to shape our identity as a church and call us to deeper spiritual formation. Our lives become "future-present" as we experience the fulfillment promised in Christ for which we were created.[6]

These are high expectations for the church's worship, but as my friend and I discovered, it is often the case that a Christian congregation finds itself beyond time, where past, present, and future are all transformed in the power of the Spirit.

There are many in the church alumni association who perceive Lord's Day worship to be the same old thing, Sunday after Sunday, but this is certainly not the case. No two gatherings of the assembly are the same because we humans and our circumstances change from day to day, week to week. More important, the substance of the Sunday celebration changes from week to week, season to season. Liturgical theologian Gordon Lathrop helps to explain the uniqueness of each celebration by noting the ways its words, actions, songs, and context are all caught up in each unrepeatable event. He focuses on the unique "juxtapositions" that make up each assembly's gathering and insists that in these juxtapositions the Spirit is at work. In a book titled *Holy Things* Lathrop describes their working this way:

> The Sunday meeting of Christians, no matter what the denominational tradition, has focused around certain things: primarily a book, a water

pool, bread and wine on a table; and secondarily fire, oil, clothing, a chair, images, musical instruments. These things are not static, but take on meaning in action as they are used, especially as they are intentionally juxtaposed. . . . Start with the simple things, the common human materials, then see how communal meaning occurs as these things are juxtaposed to each other and gathered together with speech about the promise of God. In this way, the assembly and the materials it uses become a rich locus of meaning, casting light on all common life and summed up in the shorthand of such technical words as "baptism" and "eucharist."[7]

The juxtapositions of *this* Scripture with *this* water and *this* meal in *this* place at *this* time with *this* gathered assembly make each celebration a wholly new creation. The fourfold pattern of the *ordo*—gathering, service of the Word, the Eucharist, sending—serves to order the church's time even while its movements guarantee lively juxtapositions week by week. Each celebration, each set of juxtapositions, is marked by paradox and ambiguity, new patterns alongside the old, and old patterns used in fresh ways and in combinations that are ever new, through which the Spirit of God may speak. This is our promise and our hope.

There is one aspect of time that is often absent from discussions of times and seasons. That is the reality of time within worship itself—the ticking clock, the moments and movements, and the spaces in between. If worship truly lies at the intersection of time and eternity, then worship that adheres meticulously to the clock, never taking longer than the usual one scheduled hour, is bound to miss the point.

Don Saliers grapples with this problem by telling of overhearing a conversation as people left worship on a Sunday morning. One worshiper turned to another and asked, "Whatever happened to awe?" Saliers says that though the service had been fairly typical, it contained little or no indication that worshipers understood themselves to be in the presence of an awe-inspiring God.[8]

Worshipers can't make the connection between awe and worship, Saliers says, without language and images; he describes awe as the "awakening to the reality to which our language refers."[9] Such awakening takes time. There is a purposeful but unhurried pace that is natural to worship. Worship that honors God and ushers worshipers into the divine presence takes as long as it takes. As we consider days, weeks, and seasons, it is well to remember that within that framework the movements of the *ordo* are made up of moments that, when allowed their natural flow, can awaken us to the awe of being in God's presence.

## At the Intersection of Time and Eternity

All of the church's celebrations are centered on Christ, as the shape of the weekly and yearly cycles demonstrate by recounting the stories of Christ.[10] Christians have always gathered on Sunday—the first day of the week, the Lord's Day, the day of Jesus' resurrection—to remember Jesus, his words and deeds, and share a meal. More than that, they have recalled to one another Jesus' triumph over death and God's work in raising Jesus from the dead. So Christians have gathered on the first day of the week to tell the stories of faith, to break bread and encounter the risen Lord. Christians continue to gather so that Christ may be "made known to them" in story and "in the breaking of the bread" (Luke 24:35) and to celebrate that they, too, are being raised with Christ. Today many congregations have recovered the unity of Word and Table, with Scripture, preaching, and Eucharist celebrated each Lord's Day. The fourfold pattern of gathering, service of the Word, Eucharist, and sending marks these gatherings.

Sometimes the Lord's Day is referred to as the Eighth Day. This recalls the six days of creation, the seventh day of rest, and the new creation inaugurated in Christ's resurrection: the eighth day. The first day of the week is also the eighth day: the first day of the new creation. This is why many baptismal fonts are eight-sided, to mark our baptism as entry into the new creation. Thus all time is reoriented in Christ, and each Sunday is considered a "little Easter." Throughout the year each Sunday's celebration will reflect the character of the liturgical season. Even so, during Lent when celebrations are more subdued, Sundays are not part of the penitential season. The forty days of Lent are calculated by using weekdays and Saturdays, but not Sundays, which maintain their place as the church's weekly festival of resurrection, where the whole gospel is celebrated.

The church's timekeeping is shaped by a schedule of readings from Scripture, the Revised Common Lectionary. Developed by the ecumenical Consultation on Common Texts, the Lectionary has received wide acceptance and is recommended by all of the denominations represented in this study. The Lectionary consists of a three-year calendar of readings for each Lord's Day and other festivals centered around the life, ministry, death, and resurrection of Jesus Christ. Each Lord's Day's readings include Old Testament, Psalm, Gospel, and Epistle readings. Sunday by Sunday, season by season, the church encounters God in Christ, to whom Scripture points. Given that for most people, worship is the most likely place to encounter Scripture, the church acts on God's promise that when Christians gather, the power of the

Holy Spirit makes Christ present among them.[11] With this hope in mind, we will explore the church's seasons and celebrations.

## Celebrations of Incarnation: Advent, Christmas, Epiphany

In its celebration of the incarnation, the church marks the ultimate fulfillment of God's saving purpose that begins with the birth of Jesus. It is helpful to look carefully at the celebration of Christmas, as the central organizing event of the Advent/Christmas/Epiphany cycle in order to then consider how the seasons of preparation and revelation flow from it. From the dawn of creation, the saving purposes of God have been at work, first in the people of Israel and now in the advent of the Christ child, God-with-us. The Gospel of John proclaims, "The Word became flesh and lived among us, . . . full of grace and truth" (John 1:14). "What we pay homage to at Christmas, therefore, is that *the ultimate fulfillment of God's saving purpose begins with the birth of Jesus, the messianic Savior.* God's only son is born among us in order to save the world. This is the message of Christmas."[12]

With Christmas as the center point of this cycle of celebrations, the church begins with a season of preparation during the four weeks of Advent. The natural mood of this season is preparation and anticipation for the coming of Christ, not just as a babe in the manger but also as the One who is to come. Advent directs our attention to the promised return of Christ to judge and reign over all things. During Advent we are acutely aware that we live in "in-between" times, in the time of "already but not yet." In the coming of the Christ child and all we know of his life, ministry, and ultimate triumph, the church awaits the fulfillment of all that God has promised. The cry of this season is "Come, Lord Jesus, Come!"

The colors for the season of Advent are purple and increasingly blue, the colors of repentance and preparation. In the northern hemisphere, this season occurs during the darkest days of the year. Thus the four Sundays of the season are marked by increasing light as the church looks forward to the "Light of the World." The Advent wreath, a fairly recent symbol for the season, depicts this movement with the lighting of an additional candle each Sunday. It is wise for churches to refrain from using Christmas decorations or singing Christmas carols during Advent, but rather to heighten the anticipation of Christ's coming by the gradual increase of light. The surrounding culture insists on celebrating the commercial season of Christmas from early fall onward, but the church should resist this pressure. The blues and purples of dusk and dawn make us long for the coming light. And so we gather to celebrate the presence of the one who is coming. The church's very act of worship is witness both to the world's need and to the promise of God's fulfillment. "Christians do not celebrate the liturgy nor keep the seasons in a vacuum. Rather, the readings, preaching, and singing, the greeting of peace, thanksgiving at table, and sharing of the supper take place in a world still yearning for that time when 'nation shall not lift up sword against nation' (Isa. 2:4)."[13] The celebration of Advent is countercultural, as are its central themes.

At Bethlehem Lutheran in Saint Cloud, the pastors and worship leaders admit that the Sunday morning schedule is demanding. "It seems frantic— go-go-go-go-go. There's not a moment to catch a breath," says Pastor Steve Cook. There is a Saturday evening service and then three services each Sunday morning, each with a lot of music. And there is an educational hour sandwiched in between. Especially during Advent the stress was felt by everyone. "Advent has become Christmas," says Rachel Nelson. "Everyone is struggling and stressed out. *This* is a place where people come for peace. Advent is a time of preparation." The pastors, musicians, and educational leaders wanted to relieve some of the stress of the weeks leading up to Christmas. But more than that, they understood the church's way of keeping time as countercultural and looked for a way to embody that in worship. Several years ago, after much discussion they introduced the practice of keeping silence during Advent worship, a practice they continue to treasure. The weeks leading up to Advent were filled with planning and preparing the congregation for this new practice. Contemporary music leader Brenda Handel-Johnson says, "The idea of being countercultural challenged people's thinking. But we said, There are reasons why this is worth trying. Can we take time to just sit? Will people get it?" Everyone wondered how they would teach silence.

The week before the first Sunday in Advent, the lead pastor Dee Pederson led an orientation to their Advent practice of silence, and notices were printed in the bulletin all during Advent. Normally the doors between the gathering space and the worship space are open in welcome, but during Advent they remained closed. People entered in silence. Even the procession was silent, except for a rhythmic bell tone. It was difficult to abstain from music at the beginning of worship. Some said it was "like giving up your baby" not to have music, but in the end people agreed. "We need something more austere. People are constantly bombarded by aural stimulation. We need to sit in silence," says Brenda.

The people of Bethlehem Lutheran have come to treasure this season of time outside of time and the practice of silence that announces it.

On December 25 and the evening before, the anticipation of Advent gives way to the thrill of Christmas, a season of twelve days until the arrival of the feast of Epiphany. Most of us know the "Twelve Days of Christmas"

Bethlehem Lutheran Church, Saint Cloud, Minnesota. Photo by author.

only as a song (and not a well-beloved song at that). The busyness and preparation for Christmas Day may have left us too excited or too exhausted to take much pleasure in the thought of twelve more days. How might our celebrations change if we took the twelve days of Christmas to heart, rather than cramming all of our celebrations into one day? What might happen if we savored the unfolding of the incarnation right through until January 6? Now is the time for light-filled sanctuaries ringing with carols, for Christmas gatherings and gift giving. Caroling parties and services of lessons and carols are especially appropriate for this season. The Light of the world has come! The mystery of the incarnation, God's own entering into the life of the world as a human, is before us. With the angels' announcement of peace on earth, the mission of Christ is known from the beginning. And so we celebrate for twelve days. Come to think of it, are twelve days really enough?

Throughout the twelve days of Christmas, the church celebrates the coming of the Savior of the world. At Epiphany we celebrate the manifestation of Christ's glory to all. The Christmas stories recount Christ's initial coming in human form. Epiphany, which means "appearance" or "manifestation," celebrates the revelation of God to the world in the person of Jesus of Nazareth. Events in which this manifestation took place include the coming of the magi, the baptism of Jesus, and Jesus' miracle at the wedding feast at Cana.

Tustin Presbyterian Church, Tustin, California. Photo by Helen Anderson. Used with permission.

During this season the colors of white and gold dominate. Light continues to increase, with the addition of more lights and candles. Christmas decorations remain in place, and a Twelfth Night party the night before Epiphany Sunday is in order. We have seen how Tustin Presbyterian "dresses the worship space" for the seasons. At Christmas the decorations are especially lavish and communicate the festive intention of the season.

Celebrations of the Resurrection: Lent, Easter, Pentecost

The Easter cycle of the liturgical calendar includes Lent, Easter, and Pentecost and is described as moving "from the ashes of death to the fire of the Spirit."[14] It is useful once again to consider the central celebration for this season and then to see how the seasons coming before and after Easter are integral to it. The events of Holy Week, especially the cross and resurrection, are emphasized throughout this cycle, which includes the six Sundays in Lent, seven Sundays in Eastertide, and the one Sunday of Pentecost. "We observe Lent in anticipation of the resurrection, and we celebrate Easter [while] remembering the cost of the cross's life-giving victory."[15]

The season of Lent began as a season of preparation for Easter, especially for those seeking baptism. We too are reminded of our baptism, when a cross was traced on our drenched forehead, perhaps with oil. But at the beginning of Lent on Ash Wednesday, the cross is traced in ashes as someone says, "You are dust and to dust you shall return." We are called to think of a day in the future when the cross will again identify each of us as a sheep of Christ's fold, a lamb of Christ's flock, and a sinner of Christ's own redeeming.[16] Even so, the new birth—the gift of grace—calls us to live by faith in the present moment.

The color for Lent is purple, indicating repentance, and appropriate Lenten practices include the uncluttering of our lives to make room for the work of the Spirit in us, to commit to a life of prayer, and to engage in intentional acts of kindness. In Lent we pause to learn again what it means to be a follower of Christ. "The liturgies throughout Lent try to pry loose our fingers, one by one, from presumed securities and plunge us into unknown baptismal waters, waters that turn out to be not only our death tomb, but surprisingly [also] our womb of life. Rather than falling back into nothingness, we fall back on everlasting arms. Death? How can we fear what we have already undergone in baptism?"[17] The persistent confrontation with death is a recurring theme during Lent, one of its striking countercultural features in the midst of a culture where denial of death is an all-consuming enterprise.

Worship spaces show little of the decorative flair that has marked the previous seasons. At Saint Stephen's Episcopal Church in Richmond, the customary fresh-flower decorations in all of the worship spaces are dispensed with. The children and their families who worship in Palmer Hall make a great to-do of this fact, reminding each other why during Lent the vases contain bare sticks and branches rather than colorful blossoms. They solemnly remove all the bells from their worship space, packing them away until Easter.

Passion/Palm Sunday, Maundy Thursday, and Good Friday take us to the depths of Christ's passion. At Saint Stephen's, Holy Week observances involve everyone, especially the young people. On Good Friday the youth lead the whole congregation in the stations of the cross, retelling the events of Christ's death, for which they use the entire church building and campus.

Saint Stephen's and many like it embrace the dual themes of Palm/ Passion Sunday. They know that skipping from the palm parade of Palm Sunday to Easter without including the story of the passion means overturning the deepest meanings of our redemption. The passion story is told in its fullness, along with and in contrast to the "Hosannas" of the palm parade. For those who cannot attend other Holy Week services, the dual theme of Palm/ Passion Sunday is essential.

In the ancient church, Easter celebrations were the high point of the church's year, celebrated with an all-night vigil that included the lighting of the Christ candle, Scripture readings that tell the story of salvation, the baptism of new Christians, and the celebration of the Eucharist. In recent decades many congregations have shown increasing interest in celebrations of the Easter vigil.

At Saint Stephen's, after much anticipation and waiting, the Easter Vigil is here! The font is brimming with water! The table is ready for the rich food of bread and wine. Candles are lighted, and we settle in again to hear God's saving acts. The great alleluias ring out, bells peal, and we are welcomed and washed and fed. Death has been banished and new life springs forth in the resurrection of Christ. "Easter is not simply the miracle of a dead person raised from a grave, but a celebration of power that can shatter death in order that people can freely serve the God of life. . . . Resurrection shouts 'no' to everything in our world that works against God's will, and 'yes' to God's victory."[18]

The colors of Eastertide are again white and gold, with shimmering fabrics finding a particularly appropriate place. And it will take all of Easter's fifty days to tell the story of the empty tomb and life begun anew. The empty tomb shows us an empty place, a new openness to the Spirit's working.

The events of Pentecost, inaugurated through the coming of the Holy Spirit, transformed Jesus' followers into Christ's witnesses throughout the world. In the power of the Spirit, this band of ordinary women and men became extraordinary announcers of the new order of creation established in Christ's name. "At the outset, the newborn church immediately tumbled out into the streets to witness to God's mighty works in the languages of people all over the world. By the end of the story, a tiny, Spirit-filled community of faith that broke from its present order has spread across the continents with incredible power to bring new things into being. With the gift of the Spirit, all things are possible."[19]

Symbols for Pentecost include wind and fire, and the color for the day is red. At ChristChurch Presbyterian, as in many congregations, everyone wears red, and the sanctuary is decked with red streamers, banners, paraments, and

Saint Stephen's Episcopal Church, Richmond, Virginia. Photo by Sarah Bartenstein. Used with permission.

tablecloths. All these things and more remind the church that the Spirit who empowered Christ to love enemies, heal the sick, welcome the children, and teach a new way of faithfulness is the same Spirit who empowers the church today. The witness of Lent, Easter, and Pentecost is the call to life in the Spirit, a life opened to all humanity through the life, death, and resurrection of Jesus Christ.

## Between the Seasons: Ordinary Time

From the Sunday following Pentecost until the first Sunday of Advent, and then from the Sunday following Epiphany until Ash Wednesday, the church keeps what is known as Ordinary Time. Though this term may evoke a "ho-hum" response, it is not intended to suggest that nothing of importance is taking place. During Ordinary Time the Sunday celebration is the principal focus of the church's worship. The Scripture passages that guide Lord's Day worship are focused on the ministry of Christ, on the Epistles of Paul and John, and on Old Testament texts. Worship is expected to follow a predictable or "ordinary" pattern, including the Lord's Prayer, Doxology, Creed, Kyrie, Gloria, Alleluia, Eucharist, and prayers inviting the congregation to "Lift up your hearts." "The Sundays of Ordinary Time celebrate the good news of Christ's death and resurrection, and the unfolding presence of the new creation. Ordinary Time presents us with an ongoing opportunity to witness to the living Lord who makes all things new."[20] The color of Ordinary Time is green, marking it as a time for growth.

The celebration of time in the church is never "ordinary" in the usual sense of that word. The church is always celebrating the extraordinary, surprising, life-changing deeds of God's power. The more our celebrations make these deeds visible and audible, season by season, through the architecture, environment, action, word, and song of the congregation, the more their extraordinary qualities will be made visible and audible to all who gather for worship. The more the seasons can speak their distinctive word to the gathered assembly, the more the countercultural message of Christ's redemption can be heard by the world to which we are called to bear witness. The celebrations of the church, season by season, help to fulfill the twin tasks of the church: to deepen the capacity for the church and its people to declare the glory of God, and to broaden the invitation to the world to join in giving God praise.

We conclude this chapter with a summation by Gordon Lathrop. In the face of the forgetfulness of the present age—forgetfulness of the cosmic and natural rhythms that shape the days and seasons, forgetfulness of the primordial events that have shaped human life, forgetfulness of the redemptive acts that have brought the Christian community into existence—the act of Lord's Day worship is a radical countercultural event.

> So after the week is over, before the new week begins, on a day all Christianity has set, at a time my community has determined, I come into church. Just by doing that, I am given a rhythm in time, a way to mark change and flow in my days, a simple communal calendar in which to insert my own experience of time. Merely keeping that time with others, I make a courageous statement in the face of modern forgetfulness. But because this time is a time for meeting, by coming I am inserted into the primary theology of the liturgy. The scheduled patterns of the meeting propose that time itself is held in a larger pattern of grace.[21]

The symbolic language of the church's calendar orients the church to the stories of God's redemption and to its ultimate fulfillment. Learning to "read" this language will strengthen the ways worship shapes and expresses the church's countercultural identity.

## Ideals and Questions for Discussion

*Choose two or three questions that are important for your congregation.*

1. *Ideal:* The patterns of worship are intended to follow a predictable pattern (the *ordo*) of gathering, service of the Word, Eucharist, sending. The juxtaposition of these four movements within the seasons of the church year, guided by the lectionary, makes worship endlessly variable.

   *Describe* the ways worship is the same week by week. Describe the ways worship is ever new because of the changing seasons and the changing lives of those who assemble.

   *Explain how* these similarities give worship its stability. Explain how the changes keep worship fresh.

   *Describe* the ways worship is unpredictable and perhaps unsettling. Describe the ways worship is predictable and perhaps boring.

   *Explain how* boring or unpredictable worship obscures or distorts the gospel.

   *Imagine* ways worship might better reflect the traditional *ordo* and thus be more predictable. Imagine ways worship might be enlivened and boredom avoided by attention to the seasons and lectionary texts.

2. *Ideal:* Worship exists at the intersection of time and eternity, awakening in worshipers a sense of awe and wonder.

   *Describe* the aspects of worship that awaken in you a sense of awe and wonder.

*Explain how* awe and wonder are evoked and expressed in worship.

*Imagine* possible ways worship might more fully evoke awe and wonder.

3. *Ideal:* Worship "takes as long as it takes" and is distorted by inordinate attention to time limits for the length of portions of worship and the service as a whole.

*Describe* timekeeping in worship in your congregation. Describe the "feel" of time. Does time feel rushed or sluggish?

*Explain how* the use of time supports discernment of God's presence in worship. Explain how the use of time interferes with encounter with God.

*Imagine* ways the congregation might use time that would enhance the worship of God.

4. *Ideal:* Advent is "a season to recollect the hope of the coming of Christ, and to look forward to the Lord's coming again."[22]

*Describe* the congregation's Advent celebrations.

*Explain how* these celebrations help the congregation recollect the hope of the coming of Christ. Explain how the celebrations distract or avoid hope. Explain how the celebrations point toward Christ's coming again. Explain how the celebrations distract from or avoid Christ's coming again.

*Imagine* celebrations of Advent that support the congregation's hope for Christ's coming again.

5. *Ideal:* Christmas is "a celebration of the birth of Christ."[23]

*Describe* the congregation's celebrations of the birth of Christ.

*Explain how* these celebrations draw the congregation into the joy of Christ's birth.

*Imagine* celebrations of Christmas in which Christ's birth is the focus.

6. *Ideal:* Epiphany is "a day for commemorating God's self-manifestation to all people."[24]

*Describe* the congregation's celebration of Epiphany.

*Explain how* these celebrations commemorate God's self-manifestation to all people.

*Imagine* celebrations of Epiphany in which God's self-manifestation is the focus.

7. *Ideal:* Lent is "a season of spiritual discipline and preparation, beginning with Ash Wednesday, anticipating the celebration of the death and resurrection of Christ."[25]

*Describe* the congregation's observance of Ash Wednesday.

*Explain how* these observances begin the congregation's spiritual disciplines.

*Imagine* ways to observe Ash Wednesday that support the beginning of spiritual disciplines.

*Describe* the congregation's Lenten practices.

*Explain how* these practices prepare the congregation for Holy Week and Easter. Explain how the practices might distract the congregation from spiritual preparation.

*Imagine* congregational practices that might better prepare the congregation for Holy Week and Easter.

8. *Ideal:* Holy Week is "a time of remembrance and proclamation of the atoning suffering and death of Jesus Christ."[26]

*Describe* the congregation's Holy Week observances.

*Explain how* these practices enable the congregation to remember and proclaim the atoning suffering and death of Christ. Explain how the practices might distract or avoid Christ's suffering and death.

*Imagine* Holy Week practices that might strengthen the congregation's remembrance and proclamation of Christ's suffering and death.

9. *Ideal:* Easter is "the day of the Lord's resurrection and the season of rejoicing which commemorates his ministry until his Ascension."[27]

*Describe* the congregation's celebrations of Easter and all of Eastertide.

*Explain how* these celebrations proclaim the Lord's resurrection and draw the congregation into rejoicing all season long. Explain how these celebrations might distract or shorten the season of proclamation and rejoicing.

*Imagine* ways of celebrating Easter and Eastertide that might more clearly proclaim the Lord's resurrection and sustain rejoicing throughout the season.

10. *Ideal:* The Day of Pentecost is "the celebration of the gift of the Holy Spirit to the Church."[28]

*Describe* the congregation's celebrations of Pentecost.

*Explain how* these celebrations focus the congregation's attention on the gift of the Holy Spirit to the church. Explain how these practices might distract or interrupt the congregation's focus on the gift of the Holy Spirit.

*Imagine* ways of celebrating Pentecost that draw the congregation into participating in the gift of the Holy Spirit to the church.

11. *Ideal:* Ordinary Time is made up of two periods between the beginning and ending of the other seasons. During Ordinary Time the celebration of the Lord's Day, Sunday, is primary.

*Describe* the congregation's practices during the two periods of Ordinary Time.

*Explain how* these practices call the congregation's attention to the primacy of the Sunday gathering around Word and Table. Explain how these practices might distract the congregation from the Sunday gathering.

*Imagine* ways of gathering during Ordinary Time that might strengthen the congregation's attention to the Sunday gathering around Word and Table.

Chapter 7

# Proclaiming God's Praise

## Liturgical Speech

*Religious language begins in lively metaphor, babbling a vision, exploding with ecstasy, nurturing human community. Indeed a believer hopes that such speech originates in God's own creative power.*

*Gail Ramshaw*[1]

*O*f all the symbolic languages of worship, actual words, sentences, and stories deserve careful attention. Words have a way of shaping the other liturgical languages by framing and interpreting events as they take place. At the same time, words take on new meanings through the unique role they play in the actions of worship. In this chapter we will explore the various ways language is used in worship, the ways the use of language both shapes and is shaped by other liturgical languages.

Steve Cook, pastor at Bethlehem Lutheran, is a storyteller. In his preaching, biblical stories come alive, drawing the congregation into the stories. At the annual Easter Vigil, Steve involves the whole congregation, especially the children. Scripture for the Vigil is extensive, reviewing the whole of salvation history. Children, youth, and adults enact the stories of creation, Noah's flood, the binding of Isaac, the Israelites' release from slavery, Ezekiel's valley of dry bones, the deliverance of Jonah, and the passion and resurrection of Jesus. In this congregation, brimming with talent, these stories come to life and provide language for speaking of God's saving intentions. This community of faith finds its place in these stories in such a way that they become their own story.

All of the language for worship has its roots in biblical story. Worship is a kind of language school, says Ronald Byars, "in which the novice is repeatedly exposed to native speakers."

We learn the meaning of words like "holy," "repentance," and "justification" and phrases like "Jesus is Lord" by using them and hearing them used in various contexts. We hear them in readings from Scripture; we use them in spoken prayers, in creeds spoken or sung. We hear them sung by choirs; we sing them ourselves in hymns and psalms. The preacher tells stories, links one thing with another, shows how the biblical stories and images connect with the world. Language school. Over time, we learn the nuances of the language. We begin to "inhabit" the language. It becomes a framework through which we view and understand the larger world.[2]

This language has a long and varied history, including times such as now, when the use of the church's language for worship has been devalued, forbidden, and otherwise set aside. But we set aside this language at great peril. The things of God that the church's language communicates require the nuanced specialized vocabulary of words such as *grace* and *redemption* and *holy*. Cognitive scientists and anthropologists have long known that language shapes perception and thought. A detailed vocabulary—words that name our experience of the world—enables people to both recognize and understand their world. (Why else would Alaskan native peoples have multiple words for snow or African jungle dwellers have a similar number of words for green?) Without the church's words, our attempts to describe and communicate the experience of encounter with God would fall flat.

Does this mean that the inquirer or newcomer to Christian faith is left on one's own to figure things out? Not at all! It does mean that we keep the distinction between evangelism and Christian worship clearly in mind. In an article titled "Evangelism, Evangelization, and Catechesis," John Westerhoff offers a set of helpful distinctions.[3] *Evangelism*, he says, is what Christian people do in their daily encounters with friends, neighbors, coworkers, and family members. Christians recount their encounters with Christ and identify the church as the place where Christ can be made known. *Evangelization* is the activity of the church, making Christ known and intentionally teaching the church's language to inquirers and newcomers. *Catechesis*, which has prebaptismal and postbaptismal aspects, is a lifelong process for all Christians, a process of being formed into the likeness of Jesus Christ through the church's practices of worship, prayer, acts of justice and mercy, and more. Worship naturally includes elements of both evangelism and catechesis. It proclaims the gospel to those who may never have heard it or are hearing it anew, and it is naturally formative for the Christian life. Nevertheless, this should not prevent or divert attention from every Christian's evangelical responsibilities and the church's efforts toward evangelization. In addition, we do well to keep in mind the differences between events that are primarily evangelistic and those that are the church's worship. According to Marva Dawn,

> Worship is the language of love and growth between believers and God; evangelism is the language of introduction between those who believe and those who don't. To confuse the two and put on worship the burden of evangelism robs the people of God of their responsibility to care about the neighbor, defrauds the believers of transforming depth, and steals from God the profound praise of which [God] is worthy.[4]

It may be possible to "translate" the church's message into everyday language, but even that should be considered a kind of baby talk. Soon enough even new Christians will be eager to deepen their praise and open themselves to Christ's transforming presence with the aid of the rich vocabulary of Christian faith.

At Saint Luke's Lutheran in Park Ridge, the integration of scriptural language and metaphors throughout each service receives a lot of attention. Prayers, musical texts, and Scripture are all thoughtfully woven together into a creative whole. One Sunday in the fall, the Gospel text was the parable of the Lost Coin. Prayers, hymns, anthems, and responses all made use of the metaphors of the parable. The choir sang a moving version of "Amazing Grace." The mother of a seven-year-old named Grant e-mailed the church staff to say that on the ride home from church, the boy said to his dad, "Lost and found, like the woman in the story." He had learned the song in children's choir and made connections with the parable. The educators' and musicians' response to the mother's story was "We need to bring children into worship. You learn to worship by worshiping!" A weekly e-mail to children's choir members called "Worship Notes" helps them make these connections and also includes family discussion starters. Director of Music Ministries Anne Organ says it is one of the most enjoyable parts of including children in worship.

The language of the Christian community, especially in worship, is formative. The words, images, and metaphors we choose to call on God in praise, lament, and intercession shape our vision of God, ourselves, and the world. "While worship is, first of all, an offering of praise and thanksgiving to God, it has the effect over time of forming and shaping the worshipers in a particular orientation vis-à-vis God, the universe, and one another. Our worship tunes our perceptions and feelings."[5] Rather than beginning with those feelings and perceptions, worship calls us to begin with God. Begin with the call of Abraham, the burning bush, Mary and Martha and Lazarus, the disciples' meeting Jesus on the way. Live with those stories until they become your

Saint Luke's Lutheran Church, Park Ridge, Illinois, with Lead Pastor Stephen Larson. Photo by Mike Watson. Used with permission.

story, too, and you find yourself and the whole assembly seeing differently. Again, Byars has a word of truth for us:

> Novelty is overrated. To grow in the faith requires repeated exposure to a way of looking at the world, and that perspective is available only in Scripture. We are reminded of this in 2 Corinthians 5:16: "From now on, therefore, we regard no one from a human point of view; even though we once knew Christ from a human point of view, we know him no longer in that way."[6]

The language of the liturgy, then, takes as its starting point Scripture itself. Based on careful examination of biblical accounts of encounter with God, Russell Mitman says, "Liturgical expressions that arise organically out of the scripture texts will help to immerse people into the wonder of God's splendor because that's what the Bible story is about. . . . Worship is a counter-cultural event, and when its focus is on God, worship becomes very attractive simply because God attracts!"[7] Byars's book *What Language Shall I Borrow?* goes on to demonstrate the thoroughness with which Scripture permeates the liturgy.

Linda Keener, organist and choir director at Christ Lutheran in Richmond, Virginia, says: "Many people think repetition of the same thing leads to bore-

Saint Luke's Lutheran Church, Park Ridge, Illinois, with Director of Music Ministries Anne Organ. Photo by Mike Watson. Used with permission.

dom. But really it helps keep people focused. The bodily movement required in the liturgy adds to this." Not raised in a liturgical tradition, Linda says, "I would never go back to a nonliturgical church."

At Spanish Springs Presbyterian in Sparks, Nevada, the region is dominated by what Elder Linda Zyzdik calls "big-box" churches. The churches she has visited, she says, are "doing something different every time." At Spanish Springs, even in its storefront location, the liturgy follows the traditional pattern of the *ordo* and includes traditional prayers, hymns, and lots of Scripture. According to Linda, this kind of tradition, which follows a pattern but is always new and different, leads to a deepening of faith. Pastor Bruce Taylor and other worship leaders make sure that each Sunday's liturgy is grounded in Scripture. In addition, Bruce provides newsletter articles that further illuminate the church's worship.

While Scripture provides the starting point and primary resource for liturgical language, the liturgy requires other language as well. Each congregation

Spanish Springs Presbyterian Church, Sparks, Nevada. Photo by Doug Ramseth. Used with permission.

has its own native language, drawn from its history, heritage, and life together. A community would be shortsighted indeed to ignore the congregation's own words when preparing liturgical texts.

The Directory for Worship of the Presbyterian Church (U.S.A.) gives helpful guidance, calling attention to "authentic and appropriate language" for worship:

> The historical and cultural use of language proves to be authentic when it reflects the biblical witness to God in Jesus Christ. Language proves to be appropriate when a worshiping community can claim it as its own when offering praise and thanksgiving to God. Appropriate language by its nature
>
> a. is more expressive than rationalistic,
> b. builds up and persuades as well as informs and describes,
> c. creates ardor as well as order, [and]
> d. is the utterance of the whole community of faith as well as the devotion of individuals.
>
> Appropriate language seeks to recognize the variety of traditions which reflect biblical truth authentically in their own forms of speech and action. In doing so the church honors and properly uses the language of the tradi-

tion. The church is, nonetheless, free to be innovative in seeking appropriate language for worship. While respecting time-honored forms and set orders, the church may reshape them to respond freely to the leading of God's Spirit in every age.[8]

Both form and freedom, tradition and creative innovation, are respected here, called upon to serve the assembly's expressions of praise to God.

## Language—Spoken and Heard, Not Written and Read

Of all the languages of human communication—gesture, music, architecture, the arts, and so forth—we humans have been most successful in learning to preserve speech. Our written languages take the fleeting spoken word and preserve it in pictographs, alphabets, and audio recordings that endure across time, a skill that has brought many blessings. We have the ability to be in conversation with people from other places and times, to engage with perspectives different from our own, and thus to be challenged and enriched. But written language carries risks as well as benefits. Written language brings with it the ability to take words out of their original context, leaving behind much of their communicative intent. It is possible that in the process much of the "living mystery" of language is left behind, especially in worship.[9] The risks of decontextualization that come with every written text are heightened in Scripture and the heritage of the liturgy.

The spoken, written, read words of the liturgy were never meant to dominate the other liturgical languages. In fact, the language of the liturgy is particularly vulnerable when isolated from its enacted communal context. We have noticed that many mainline denominations have produced liturgical texts over recent decades, but rather than assume that these books contain all that is needed for the community's worship, many of the worship books are supported by additional resource materials that make plain the place of words in the midst of the enacted liturgical context.[10] Though in the past it may have been assumed that the liturgy was mostly about language—Scripture perfectly read, prayers precisely spoken, doctrinal statements accurately repeated—that is no longer the case. As Ostdiek reminds us, "Liturgical speech does not stand alone. It has its fullest meaning only in the context of the entire liturgical event, when it names and sums up all [that] the liturgical languages wish to convey to us."[11] The words of the liturgy may well have been written and perhaps published with the intention that they be read during a liturgical event, but the reading of the words is not the point. All the words of the liturgy, including the printed words, serve the assembly's full, conscious, active participation. Printed texts, as we have seen, have both the advantage of preservation and the disadvantage of being separated from the events that gave rise to them. The availability of these texts for present-day use indicates that they should not be disconnected from the here-and-now worship of the assembly but rather that they enrich it.

Those who lead worship—read Scripture, speak prayers, pronounce blessings—take on an awesome responsibility and have "a significant influence on the quality and meaning of the whole service and, possibly, on the lives of participants in that service."[12] Worship leaders must enter into the world and words of another, leaving their own words behind in order to present a fresh rendering of an ancient text. When Scripture is read, it is somehow "brought back to life" in the mouth of the reader.[13] That is why much of Scripture and most all denominationally published liturgical texts are written for the ear. Rather than carefully constructed persuasive essays, liturgical texts are intended to be *heard*, with the understanding that worship is an event: an enacted, aural event, a "doing" with words. When the words of worship, no matter how carefully spoken and accurate, fail to bring the text to life for the present context, worship becomes flat and lifeless, "draping the whole occasion with a pall of indifference and unimportance."[14] In most congregations there are leaders and members who, with a little coaching and encouragement, can become effective worship leaders, and resources for use in training are available from almost every denomination. In worship, by the power of the Holy Spirit, God is present and active in our prayers, Scripture, and blessings to form a people in the likeness of Jesus Christ. It is the role of worship leaders to invite the assembly into the dynamic center of God's presence and action.

At Saint Luke's Lutheran Church the assisting minister, a nonordained member of the congregation, leads the prayers of the people. Persons who serve in this way say that the process of writing prayers and leading the congregation in prayer is formative for them. The Schaffer family, Mom Kim and Dad Mark and their teenaged twins, Trevor and Sara, say they are all involved in leading worship. "We read lessons and serve communion," say the twins. "You are there to share that meal and be a vessel for Christ. Sometimes we are crucifer and get to carry the cross in procession. It is an awesome honor. When we read, we get the lessons ahead of time so we can be prepared." All the leaders in this congregation agree. Children and young people are regularly included in worship and in the leadership of worship.

Saint Luke's Lutheran Church, Park Ridge, Illinois. Photo by Mike Watson. Used with permission.

## The Story of the Redemption of Creation

The Christian story is just that: a story—a narrative account of events, actions, and responses, along with their accompanying emotions and feelings. Although many stories in Scripture make up the Christian story, it is, in reality, one very long yet coherent story in which God initiates encounter with the chosen people in order to bring about redemption and blessing for all the families of the earth. It is this story that the whole of the liturgy is aiming to proclaim. The story centers on Christ and, with the aid of the Revised Common Lectionary, is told season by season, year by year, in all its splendid variety. The story of God's way with humankind is told, beginning at the dawn of creation, through the accounts of the patriarchs and matriarchs of Israel, their desert wanderings led by Moses, the anguish and restoration told by the prophets, and reaching its pinnacle in the life, ministry, death, and resurrection of Jesus Christ. "God in Christ is the Subject of worship, and the divine-human encounter begins with God. . . . People come expecting to hear what *God* will be saying and to encounter what *God* will be doing in the worship event. The journey toward the sacred . . . is a yearning somewhere somehow to be touched and handled by things unseen."[15]

One of the most common ways to tell the Christian story is metaphor. The use of metaphor in liturgy (or in any setting) begins with rejecting the notion that words are "merely labels" and that there is a one-to-one correspondence between each word and that to which it refers. Rather than unambiguous descriptions of reality, words function in multiple ways at the same time, with nuances of meaning revealed in the many ways words may be combined. Metaphors lay one idea or image alongside another in ways that make new meaning and illuminate our perception. By showing us something old and something new, we see both afresh. For example, when the church declares that we are buried with Christ in baptism and are raised to walk in newness of life (Rom. 6), it is not a literal burial of which we speak (although the practice of baptism by immersion is intended to resemble burial). Rather, it is a metaphor wherein baptism and Christ's own death and burial are laid side by side in a way that illuminates the meaning of baptism. "Metaphor does not label: it connects in a revolutionary way. Metaphor is not merely an image, the look-alike, the reflection in the mirror. Rather, the metaphor forms a comparison where none previously existed. Metaphor alters perception by superimposing disparate images."[16]

The liturgy is intentionally saturated with metaphors drawn from the stories of Scripture and is especially effective in conveying its new vision when the language for a particular gathering is integrated, when repeated metaphors connect with one another throughout the entire service. Beginning with the images found in the biblical texts for the day, prayers, hymns, litanies, acclamations, and sermons can be found or constructed so that the message of Scripture permeates all of the liturgy's language. Thus a set of particular liturgical texts can be organic, weaving and reweaving themes and metaphors into a rich tapestry of liturgical language. "All the expressions reinforce one another so that the whole is more than the sum of the parts."[17] At the same time it is important to set the old alongside the new, the familiar alongside the unfamiliar in ways that both deepen faith and enliven insight.

The unique context of each worship event is evident in the language of the liturgy. Careless use of language in worship can wound and alienate those we are trying to serve. Therefore the language used in the liturgy considers carefully those who gather and their particular needs. The language of the liturgy will always strive to help all feel included—male and female, those who are celebrating and those who are grieving, the poor and powerless, the advantaged and powerful, the ill and the healthy.[18]

We have already spoken of the necessity of language school for understanding the liturgy, and it is this metaphorical language that is the content of the curriculum. But rather than a demanding series of instructions, this language school is best attended by immersion. By regular participation in the liturgy, by listening to and participating in the stories, prayers, blessings, and acclamations of the liturgy, the assembly becomes fluent in the scripturally grounded stories and their metaphorical embellishments so that we begin to see through them into the mystery of God's saving presence. At the same time it is necessary for the assembly to provide language coaches—baptismal and membership sponsors, pastors, educators, Sunday school teachers, youth leaders, pastoral care specialists, choir leaders, and more—who can provide the lifelong catechesis necessary to Christian life and worship.

The words of worship come to life in part because of the ways each word sits next to another word, one image next to another. But words also sit in the midst of silence. Grant White claims that silence is necessary to speech:

> Silence is a necessary counterpart to speech. Just as the depth and joy of feasts cannot really be appreciated without the experience of fasting or abstinence, so too the words of the Scripture readings need to be balanced with an expectant silence that nourishes our reflection on what has been read. We need the silence to be able to hear the thundering echoes of what God is saying in and through the reading.[19]

It is not only after the reading of Scripture that silence is appropriate. Silence can be kept at the beginning and ending of a service, during prayers, after the sermon, and at other times that meet the needs of the assembly's liturgy. As we have seen, Bethlehem Lutheran used silence at the beginning of its Advent services to mark the season with calm anticipation. The appropriate length of silence will vary from congregation to congregation and from one moment to another in the service. Congregations may want to experiment with a gradual lengthening of silence so that, rather than a brief pause, silence becomes an opportunity for meditation for the whole assembly.

## The Language of the Sermon

For several hundred years, the Protestant tradition has privileged the sermon above all other types of liturgical language, and along with it an emphasis on doctrinal exactness. Ask almost any teenager about sermons she has heard, and you are likely to hear a resounding response of "Booooooooorrrrrring!" Our heritage from the sixteenth century onward has been one of elevating reason over imagination and doctrinal purity over the enchantment of the mysteries of the gospel. In a winsome book titled *Whatever Happened to Delight? Preaching the Gospel in Poetry and Parables*, preacher and poet J. Barrie Shepherd laments the state of preaching: "Why is it that so many sermons nowadays have so little genuine joy in them? Why do so many display such an absence of true beauty? Why do they seem to come across, less like a treasure hunt, more like an instruction manual, the bylaws of your condominium, or those assembly directions in four languages for whatever you just bought at the Do-It-Yourself store?"[20] Rather, says Shepherd, the sermon should be less a series of logical arguments, and more an imaginative construction,

> a weaving together of images, poetry, incidents, scenes and vignettes, along with suggestions, testimony hints from other imaginers. All of which are intended to convey not so much a well-argued and persuasive conclusion but rather an experience, an encounter with transcendence, with awe perhaps and mystery, with wonder, surprise, outrage at times and shame, above all with grace.[21]

This description of preaching corresponds well with the centrality of biblical metaphor in worship. With this as a star by which to navigate, preachers are set free to imagine and create sermons fitting for their context and engaged in the mystery of encounter with God. With time and space set aside for prayer, study, and preparation, preachers can entrust themselves to the creative leading of the Spirit. Craig Satterlee advises preachers to "trust preaching, . . . to embrace the sermon as a word from the Lord. To trust preaching is to dare to believe that God speaks in and through preaching, . . . and that what the congregation hears and experiences is the power of God to bring new life."[22] Mitman echoes a similar sentiment when he identifies "the homiletical and liturgical task before the church today: unapologetically in preaching and worship to speak and act in such ways that, although they are human words and actions, what is seen and heard is the One Word of God, Jesus Christ."[23]

At Saint Stephen's Episcopal Church in Richmond, young families worship together in Palmer Hall. Though the service as a whole is geared toward children's participation, the preaching is never dumbed down. Betsy Tyson, who coordinates the Palmer Hall services, says the sermons really inspire people: "Parents often tell me they couldn't stop talking about what was said by the preacher in worship." This engagement is supported by an openness in the prayers of the people. "There is an open honesty here," says Betsy.

Those with long experience in serving as presiders and preachers in the assembly often speak of the need for "transparency" in those roles. They are referring to the need to pray, plan, prepare, and rehearse the liturgy and the sermon so that they can get out of the way. Preachers and presiders often say, "It is not about *me*. It is about my getting out of the way so the congregation can discern the presence and activity of God in our midst." Presiders and preachers serve the gathered people and the liturgy they enact rather than themselves. The energetic calm, poise, and presence of the well-prepared presider create a place for the assembly confidently to enter into the divine-human encounter toward which all liturgy is directed.

The language of the liturgy and the language of preaching support worship leaders in this undertaking. The language of the liturgy is made up neither of slack colloquialisms nor outdated formalisms. It is filled with rich biblical images and metaphors, surrounded by clarity and winsome turns of phrase that draw us in and enlighten our vision. Rather than precise formulas and maxims worthy of a marble plaque or a card on the refrigerator door, the language of the liturgy is imaginative, creative in the ways it lays one thing next to another so that both are illuminated. Shepherd advises close attention to words and the ways they fit together: "As for words—these are the working tools of our trade. Treat them with care. Value them for their specificity; there's usually a wrong word and a right, or at least a better, word. Treasure them for their variety. There is almost always more than one good way to say a thing."[24] Relying on God's creativity implanted in humanity's own endowments, Shepherd advises turning to the *imago Dei*, the fact that we are created in God's image, for the imagination necessary for the creation of lively liturgical language.

## The Assembly's Words

Go to any church on any Sunday morning, and you will almost assuredly be handed a worship leaflet filled with printed words, many of them scripted for the congregation. In North America we assume universal literacy, and this assumption is reflected in the words we provide for congregations to say. No matter how it may appear, with important speaking parts given to worship leaders, the assembly's words are paramount, and so those who prepare words for the congregation bear tremendous responsibility to enable their full, conscious, active participation. I've always been a little jealous of Roman Catholics, Lutherans, Episcopalians, and others for their carefully prepared liturgical books. In some traditions, my own included, even when there are sanctioned liturgical books available, it is common practice to provide newly composed litanies, confessions, prayers, even "creeds" for the congregation to read together. This is intended, I am sure, to keep the liturgy "fresh" and to integrate the whole service, using images and metaphors from the day's Scripture (a highly recommended practice). However, as we have heard from Ronald Byars, "novelty is overrated." A new litany or prayer each week may actually serve to diminish the congregation's participation by requiring close attention to reading words on a page rather than praying fully, consciously, actively. Often the spoken and heard quality of these new compositions is sacrificed, so that when read aloud they seem like propositional statements. Words, as we have seen, are formative, and the assembly's words are particularly formative. A balance of both new and familiar elements allows the assembly to be both surprised by insight and invited to participate at the level of deep formation.

## Telling the Truth in Church

When was the last time you heard a testimony to Christian faith in worship? In my case this usually happens on "youth Sunday," when teenagers take charge of the service and recount ways their participation in mission trips and other youth activities has formed their faith. Otherwise, in the congregation where I worship and I suspect many others, testimony from within the assembly is almost completely absent. United Church of Christ Pastor Lillian Daniel, in a book titled *Tell It Like It Is: Reclaiming the Practice of Testimony*, describes how her congregation invited members to share their stories of faith with the whole church. She says, "Often in our congregations, beautiful stories of God float through the church unspoken."[25] In a similar book, Thomas Long quotes Dorothy Day as saying, "If I have achieved anything in my life, it is because I have not been embarrassed to talk about God."[26]

Testimony has a robust and respected place throughout Scripture, where people of faith are called to testify to God's power in their lives. As Christians tell their stories, they become known to one another and are themselves transformed. Those who testify engage in a process of reflection and clarification that changes them and their understanding of faith. Daniel writes that the practice of testimony has "open[ed] up the church, not only creating excitement in worship, but in coffee hour discussions as well. We were making new friends, hearing new stories of faith, being woken up by the Word."[27]

At Fairmont United Methodist Church in Raleigh, North Carolina, testimony is a regular part of the Sunday Night Live service. This neighborhood congregation, not far from a large state-college campus, is host to more than fifteen twelve-step meetings each week in addition to their other programs.

The Sunday evening service is called "Sunday Night LIVE—It's Biblical, Musical, Dramatic, Recovery Friendly, Compassionate, and more fun than anybody ought to be allowed to have in church!" The church bus picks up residents of a recovery program, and the sanctuary is filled with church members and twelve-step regulars. They pray, read Scripture, give testimony, and sing. Those gathered for worship, especially those seeking recovery, tell of the many ways God has blessed them. Testimonies include stories told but also songs sung and prayers prayed.

Each congregation will devise its own ways of including testimony in its gatherings, maybe as part of particular liturgical seasons, stewardship season, or in response to special events like mission trips. Whatever patterns a congregation might develop, the value of testimony is that it calls people into the larger story of God's activity in the world and in the life of the assembly.

The words of worship are intended to complement and amplify the actions of worship so that all of the liturgy's "languages" speak their harmonious word of praise to God. These words include Scripture, hymns, and other sung texts, prayers, litanies, creeds, and much more. When set alongside the actions of worship in the setting of the worship space, these words take on a depth of meaning that forms the community of faith into the body of Christ. This metaphorical and symbolic power of language is indispensible to faithful Christian worship and calls on our deepest imaginative and creative powers to choose the right words at the right time. Set the poets in your congregation to this task, and see what God has in store.

## Ideals and Questions for Discussion

*Choose two or three questions that are important for your congregation.*

1. *Ideal:* "The church continually builds upon the vocabulary of the Scriptures, expanding the treasury of language and images in order to proclaim the fullness of the triune God."[28]

   *Describe* the ways the language of Scripture is used in the worship of your congregation.

   *Explain how* the language of Scripture in prayers, preaching, and Scripture itself helps us proclaim the fullness of God. Explain how language inhibits or detracts from proclamation of the fullness of God.

   *Imagine* ways the vocabulary and images of Scripture could be more fully present in the language of the congregation's worship.

2. *Ideal:* The language of worship is appropriate when the community can claim it as its own when offering praise and thanks to God.

*Describe* the "native language" of your congregation. What words, phrases, and stories are particularly significant to the congregation and are repeated again and again?

*Explain how* these words, phrases, and stories shape the spiritual life of the congregation.

*Imagine* ways the congregation's native language could be strengthened and used more effectively.

3. *Ideal:* "Appropriate language by its nature . . . is more expressive than rationalistic" and "creates ardor as well as order."[29]

*Describe* the expressive qualities of the language for worship. Describe the rationalistic qualities of the language for worship. Describe the relationship between the two kinds of language. Describe the proportions of each in your worship.

*Explain how* the language of worship appeals to the emotions as well as to the intellect.

*Imagine* the ideal balance between the expressive and the rationalistic qualities of language.

4. *Ideal:* In the worship of God there is harmony between the words of worship and the actions of worship.

*Describe* the relationships between words and actions in worship.

*Explain how* they are in harmony. Explain how they contradict one another. Explain how they are unrelated to one another.

*Imagine* ways the language of worship and the actions of worship might be more harmonious.

5. *Ideal:* Preaching is contextual and is shaped and nourished by life in the community of faith.

*Describe* the ways preaching is shaped and nourished by your particular context.

*Explain how* this shaping is, in turn, formative for the community.

*Imagine* ways preaching might be more thoroughly grounded in the context.

6. *Ideal:* The sermon should present the gospel with simplicity and clarity, in language that can be understood by the people.

*Describe* the language of sermons in your church.

*Explain how* the gospel is presented.

*Imagine* ways preaching might more clearly present the gospel.

7. *Ideal:* The practice of testimony can provide opportunities for a variety of faith stories to be told.

*Describe* opportunities for testimony in your church.

*Explain how* these opportunities shape the life of the congregation.

*Imagine* possible opportunities for regularly including testimony in worship.

Chapter 8

# Lifting Our Voices

## Liturgical Song

*The LORD said to Moses, ". . . Now therefore write this song, and teach it to the Israelites; put it in their mouths, in order that this song may be a witness for me."*
*Deuteronomy 31:16, 19*

*The Christian church was born singing. . . . In all good hymn singing . . . we sing not alone, but in union with the whole creation and with our brothers and sisters through the ages.*
*Donald E. Saliers[1]*

*O*f all the symbolic languages of worship, none is so irresistible as music. When the music starts, we understand something that might otherwise go unnoticed. Music can still our hearts, clear our minds, focus our attention, and call us to deeper participation in the church's shared life in Christ. Music does this in an indirect way: its melodies and harmonies make direct appeal to our deepest longings. In this chapter we will highlight some of the ways music's role in worship can be clarified and thus fulfill its part in the congregation's praise.

Every Sunday evening, Pastor Steve Hickle stands on the steps of Fairmount United Methodist Church in Raleigh and plays the trumpet. As the twelve-step regulars arrive, the singing begins, and boy, do they sing! As their praises and laments and intercessions and supplications are lifted up in song, the whole assembly knows itself to be blessed, to be in the presence of God. The Lord's song is in their mouths as a witness. This congregation and many like it find their life together supported and enriched through their shared singing.

Almost every book and article about the church's worship repeats the phrase from the Vatican II documents that the worship of the assembly aims for "full, conscious, active participation" of the whole assembly.[2] One

121

principal means of participation for those gathered for worship—the people and the ministers who serve—is congregational song. The Evangelical Lutheran *Principles for Worship* makes this clear: "In the church the primary musical instrument is the human voice, given by God to sing and proclaim the word of God."[3] And, "The assembly is the primary musical ensemble, and its song is the core of all music in worship."[4] Singing is a natural, largely irrepressible human response of the experience of life. It begins with our bodies, with breathing in and breathing out, with the rhythmic beating of the heart, with the clapping of hands and stamping of feet. Music is embedded in our bodies from the moment of our birth. In addition, we are born into a social world, a world of parents, siblings, and clan where music takes up its place as a communal and social practice shared by every culture around the globe.

Music gives voice to our deepest joys and longings. Susanne Langer has observed that music, because it is nonverbal, may be a particularly accurate medium for expressing human emotions. Music sounds like feelings feel, she says.[5] This insight is described more fully by Donald Saliers:

> Whatever people can say with passion and in heightened speech they will end up singing in some form. When our language is used to move beyond the mere giving of information, we come to the threshold of song. When life is deeply felt or perceived, music gives shape and voice to the very pattern of our experienced world, through pitch, rhythm, and intensity, through lyrics and harmony. The tensions, resolutions, moods, convictions and playfulness of everyday life are translated into the patterns of sound. But so also are the deepest mysteries of love and death, of loss and recovery of the sense of life. So the act of singing together of life lived and felt binds heart and mind with ordered sound.[6]

Music engages our whole being, body and soul, heart and mind, individual and community in the shared act of, as Saliers puts it, "singing our lives."

Music in worship, with the whole assembly as its primary ensemble, draws us into the presence of God through our embodied, communal participation.[7] According to Saliers, there are three different levels of worship participation, all of which are affected by music. First there is a level of basic participation, doing all the things the assembly does—standing, sitting, singing, reading, praying, participating in the rites themselves. It is "participation in and through the communicative power of the visual, the acoustical, and the oral—which, of course, includes silence—the tactile, the gestural, the movement, the dance."[8] The more thoroughly the assembly participates at this level, the greater the possibility that worshipers will be open to the other two deeper levels of participation. The second level of participation is as the *church,* as those called in Christ's name who recognize one another as brothers and sisters. Typical social gatherings include those who are like us, who share our values, worldview, and lifestyle. In worship all of that is set aside as we gather with all whom God has called: past, present, and future.

> Our natural bent is to stick with those we know and the comfort zone, as it were. But the Gospel calls us to be in a community of people in continuity with all those who have gone before, and in continuity with those yet unborn, and in continuity with the poor and the unlike. . . . It's because we're willing to weep with those who weep, and rejoice with those who rejoice, even with those we shall never meet. And we can weep, and you can rejoice, because we have learned the language from those who have done it before; we are part of a continuum of faith.[9]

This level of participation goes further than "friendliness" or "community." It begins there, surely, but extends to all who weep and all who rejoice.

The third level of liturgical participation is something we have talked about before, in chapter 2: participation in the divine life itself. Worship is a kind of play or dance wherein the assembly sings, prays, listens, feeds and is fed, touches and is touched, heals and is healed—all for the sake of participation in the mystery of the life of the triune God. Saliers calls it "participation in the very triune dance of glory," wherein there is "union without loss of individual identity."[10] And all of this is for the sake of the world, both as witness and as intercession. When we worship, we are showing the world what it means to enter into the dance of the divine life. Our sending out at the conclusion of the liturgy carries that divine life into the world, so that every act of justice and mercy is "in Christ's name."

These three levels of participation are evident in almost every congregation. Some show up and just go through the motions. Others participate deeply in the communal life of the congregation as an end in itself. And there are those who, through the processions, songs, prayers, stories, eating, drinking, and bathing, find themselves participating in love's dance—God, ourselves, and the world. This is God's gift to us in the liturgy. For this reason "ritual must be conceived, created, composed, and choreographed as an art of a performing assembly. The artists of ritual are not the folks up front, the multiple ministers. The artists of ritual are none other than all of the members of the assembly, including ministers."[11] Although liturgy shows many similarities with other kinds of artistic performance, it is not a performance, and the assembly is not an audience. Musical leaders as well as other leaders may play and sing and speak and act in ways that resemble concerts or plays, but their role is profoundly different. The liturgy is enacted *with* and *by* the assembly at the invitation of the triune God.

Many congregations have moved toward fuller participation through music. Global church music as well as music from various genres has greatly expanded the repertoires of many congregations as they move beyond the hymnal. In addition, newer hymnals and hymnal supplements feature much of this music. The use of more service music—sung prayers, responses, acclamations—has increased and has made a lasting contribution to the musical heritage of many congregations. According to Thomas Long,

> Vital congregations represent a trend toward the increased use of music in worship. But the shift is more than quantity. While some churches may see worship as a series of words punctuated occasionally by pieces of music—a hymn, a response, an interlude—in the vital congregations one has the sense of being carried along in the service by music, of music as the thread that ties the flow of the service together.[12]

Music used in this way not only strengthens the three levels of participation identified above. In doing so it also opens a pathway toward deep liturgical spiritual formation.

## Music and Spiritual Formation

We have explained earlier how worship both shapes and expresses what we believe about God, ourselves, and the world, and this is especially true for music. In all of the recent discussions of worship style, focused mostly on musical style, it is music's power to shape and express the Christian spiritual life that is at stake. Linda Clark says, "Style is not just a whim or fancy. . . . The style of a congregation discloses its inner, collective, spiritual world. It displays people's attitudes about and their understanding of God and people; it also communicates the appropriate relationship between the two."[13] Clark uses the term "piety" to name this inner, collective spiritual world. Piety, according to Clark, is the corporate inner life of the church, made visible in its worship, fellowship, and mission. Piety is a function of both reflective and "prereflective" assumptions and commitments about God's being and action and about the proper shape of the Christian life. Prereflective assumptions include the belief that the religious realm is more than verbal reflections. It lives at a more profound, perhaps unspoken, level for most people. "Piety grows out of the depths of people, not just their conscious minds." The choices made by church members are not limited only by considerations of what they like and what is considered conventionally attractive. "They must also decide what is *appropriate for a holy place.* . . . Ideas about God are already at work in these decisions. . . . This is as true of the decision about the paint on the walls as it is about the hymns to be sung."[14]

The Presbyterian Directory for Worship affirms that "prayer is at the heart of worship,"[15] and the church from its earliest days has declared that what we pray influences what we believe. Musician Michael Hawn reflects on the formative power of music, especially in the global church, and encourages congregations to reestablish the link between prayer and song. If, as Augustine taught, the one who sings prays twice, then this is good advice indeed. Hawn quotes Albert van den Heuvel of the World Council of Churches, who says,

> It is the hymns, repeated over and over again, which form the container of much of our faith. They are probably in our age the only confessional documents which we learn by heart. As such, they have taken the place of our catechisms. . . . There is ample literature about the great formative influence of the hymns of a tradition on its members. Tell me why you sing, and I'll tell you who you are![16]

Michael Simpson, organist and choir director at Saint Stephen's Episcopal Church in Richmond, asks, "How many sermons can you quote? Most people can quote more hymn texts. I often take time to explain to the choirs why we are singing a particular song. It informs the music-making. The reason for choral music is the *words*. The text is set in a particular way, and one's point of view is shaped by the musical setting." The joining of text and tune, then, is formative.

## What to Choose? How to Choose?

The Evangelical Lutheran *Principles for Worship* states that "music in worship carries the assembly's prayer beyond words alone. Music shapes, nurtures, and assists the prayer of God's people. . . . We seek to use as fully as possible music's ability to carry prayer, allowing prayer to find expression in its natural musical shape and flow, both with words and without words. . . . Careful thought and preparation stir the winds of creativity and strengthen the assembly's prayer."[17] What goes into the "careful thought and preparation" for music that will carry the assembly's prayer?

Let's begin with musical variety. We are what we sing, says John Witvliet, who recommends a "balanced diet" of a wide variety of music drawn from a wide variety of cultural locations and ethnic communities in all periods of history. Good music, he says, can "form us in the native prayer language of many parts of the holy, catholic church. It should include songs in a variety of emotional registers from the contemplative to the exuberant."[18] Research shows that most congregations do not have a balanced musical diet but repeat the same 100 to 125 hymns year after year.[19] As we noted in chapter 1, asking congregations to try something new in worship, especially music, may be "a third rail" of congregational life. With the spiritual formation of the congregation at stake, however, it may well be worth the risk. Recent years have seen a marked abundance of music for worship from a variety of sources. New offerings come regularly from composers and hymn writers. The riches of the global church are more and more available. The musical experimentation of the last several decades has brought a wide variety of musical genres and instrumentation to the church's attention. The church does not lack for variety in music.

Have you ever been asked to sing a familiar hymn text to an unfamiliar tune or new words with a familiar tune? Sometimes new pairings of this sort can bring flashes of insight. At other times such stunts seem to be novelty for novelty's sake. Michael Simpson strives for tune and text that are fully integrated. "Our staff discussions of the liturgy start with the theme from the Gospel texts. When we are choosing music, we ask, How do we get from the Gospel text to each part of the liturgy, including the music?"

With the formative power of music and accompanying texts in mind, it is well to evaluate whether or not a particular piece of music is "fitting." Do text and tune support one another? Does the music fit into the flow of the service, providing the right music at the right time? Does this piece serve the assembly and its liturgy? No one person's response to these questions is adequate. These questions—indeed all of the issues and questions in this book—are intended to support open and frank conversations among members of the congregation and their leaders. Standards of excellence exist for each genre and style of music, maybe not in the form of a checklist, but as a deep sense of resonance based on training and familiarity. Worship calls for the best we can offer. With the goals of bringing honor to God and sharing in the congregation's spiritual formation, musicians, pastors, educators, and congregational leaders can collaborate in effectively shaping the musical worship of the assembly.

At Saint Luke's Lutheran Church in Park Ridge, Illinois, the entire music, education, and pastoral staff meets regularly for detailed conversations and worship planning. As we have observed earlier, there is close coordination among all the program leaders with the result that congregational spiritual formation permeates the entire church. One bright fall afternoon not long

Saint Stephen's Episcopal Church, Richmond, Virginia. Photo by Sarah Bartenstein. Used with permission.

before All Saints' Day, a group of retired men and women, some of them married couples, gathered in the fellowship hall for a discussion of end-of-life issues. Pastors Stephen Larson and Kristi Weber and musician Anne Organ had spent time in preparation and deliberation for the event. Titled "Five Wishes," the pastor led the group through a discussion of how to communicate their wishes for end-of-life care, and then the pastors and musician

Saint Luke's Lutheran Church, Park Ridge, Illinois. Photo by Mike Watson. Used with permission.

Saint Luke's Lutheran Church, Park Ridge, Illinois. Photo by Mike Watson. Used with permission.

together led the group in singing and praying through the funeral service. The music was varied and the singing robust as these seasoned worshipers gave and received care in the midst of difficult subject matter. Rather than resist and avoid the topic, however, these Christians revealed a strong confidence in God's abiding care, embodied and sung in the church. The hymns they chose from the list of almost one hundred provided by musician Anne Organ were hymns of gratitude and hope. They sang their faith even, and maybe especially, in the face of death.

Expanding the musical repertoire of a congregation requires change. It requires trying new things and assessing their authenticity and appropriateness for *this* congregation at *this* time.[20] Conversations necessary for this process can be aided by keeping several things in mind. First, know the congregation. Know its history, context, and aspirations. Make times and places available for new and longtime members of the congregation to share their experiences of worship together. Come to a shared understanding of this background as you and others enter into conversations about the church's worship life. Only then will you be able to discern what is fitting for the assembly.

Learning to sing a new song may be difficult for some. It is never expected that everyone will appreciate every musical offering made in worship (or anywhere else). Rather, a generosity of spirit should permeate all of our deliberations and decisions about music (and more). But as we know, this often seems to prove difficult. Cornelius Plantinga and Sue Rozeboom remind us that our worship arises from our shared calling in Christ:

> Christians share a general view of the world and of our calling in it, namely, that the world has been created and redeemed by God, through Jesus Christ, and that those in union with Christ should "live for the praise of his glory" by "seeking first the kingdom of God" (Eph. 1:12; cf. Matt. 6:33). . . .
>
> Because of devotion to our common Lord, we may rejoice not only in our own salvation but also in the salvation of neighbors—who might express their worship, prayer, or joy in a way we wouldn't choose.[21]

They go on to articulate a set of virtues that Christians are called to demonstrate in all our dealings with one another. First of all, they say, Christians need candor, that kind of straightforward conversation that sets aside hidden agendas and destructive backbiting. Honest communication as the first step allows everyone to know where others stand so that various concerns can be addressed. It has been the premise of this book all along that Christian worship should not be evaluated by "Did you like it?" criteria. However, unless personal tastes and preferences are brought into the open, they cannot be dealt with adequately. But that is not enough, and it would be tragic if we got stuck there. Candor must move on to the virtue of hospitality, "the gracious readiness to make room for others and their interests."[22] Our interests are that the worship of the assembly in this place should honor God and call out a people for faithful service. Hospitality does not mean that we give in or give up our identity. Rather, it means that we examine the way our identity may be grounded in musical style rather than the call of Christ. We may find that our identity may be enriched by accepting, welcoming, and entertaining the views of others.[23] I have long harbored the suspicion that some church musicians, maybe especially amateur musicians who make up most of the church's music makers, are closet wannabes. The love for singing and playing never quite brought them to the brightly lighted stage of fame and acclaim, but in the church they get a taste of what it's like to be in the spotlight. I see this in myself (a trained singer past her prime) and among music makers who favor all genres of music. I sometimes wonder if the identity of performer overshadows our identity in Christ, making the virtue of hospitality even more difficult. When our identity is founded on performance of a certain style of music, frank conversations that call us to modify that part of our identity can be difficult. The virtues of candor and hospitality call us to a new level of spiritual formation.

The virtue of forbearance, "the willingness to put up with people who make us crazy,"[24] is a virtue for the long haul in liturgical renewal. This has nothing to do with "giving in" but everything to do with keeping that larger vision in view. Forbearance calls us to tolerate things we wouldn't choose for ourselves in order to move toward a more important goal, in this case the faithful worship of God by the whole assembly. In forbearance we demonstrate "goodwill toward our neighbor, a desire to see her flourish as God intended."[25]

What is at stake here in the call to embrace the virtues of candor, hospitality, and forbearance is nothing less than the shape of the Christian life itself. When we consciously practice these virtues, at least two things happen. First, we as individual Christians are formed ever more faithfully into the likeness of Christ. Second, the community of faith takes on a more Christlike way of being that perpetuates its own formation and its witness in the world. (Congregations that are continually in conflict rarely are places where ministry and mission can be energetically carried out.)

All who gather for worship would do well to give thanks to God for faithful musicians who lead them. The musician, says Paul Westermeyer, "is the steward of God's gracious gift of music. Since this gift is so powerful, the steward receives tremendous power as the deputy. The power can easily be misused for selfish ends. . . . The musician is called . . . to the paradox . . . of using it with restraint on behalf of God in Christ, from whom all blessings flow."[26]

In a sense music ties all of worship's symbolic languages together. What would a procession be without singing? What would Scripture and preaching be without the response of hymns? Musicians, in their many roles, help to shape the worshiping community in its encounter with God and express its wonder at being in God's presence. Thus music that is attentive to the unique character of the congregation and to the role that each piece of music fulfills within the whole of the liturgy serves worship's highest goals, the full-hearted praise of God.

## Ideals and Questions for Discussion

*Choose two or three questions that are important for your congregation.*

1. *Ideal:* "In the church, the primary musical instrument is the human voice, given by God to sing and proclaim the word of God."[27] And, "The assembly is the primary musical ensemble, and its song is the core of all music in worship."[28]

*Describe* the place of the human voice in the worship of your congregation. Describe the primary musical ensemble.

*Explain how* this way of including music in worship forms or perhaps malforms the congregation's spiritual life.

*Imagine* ways of including the human voice of the assembly more fully in the music for worship.

2. *Ideal:* Music gives shape and voice to the very pattern of our experienced world.

*Describe* the moods, genres, and emotions of the music used in worship.

*Explain how* these musical selections shape the congregation's perceptions of God, themselves, and the world.

*Imagine* changes in the kinds of music used in worship.

3. *Ideal:* Expanding the musical repertoire of the congregation requires hospitality, candor, and forbearance.

*Describe* the congregation's practices of hospitality, candor, and forbearance in the shaping of its musical choices.

*Explain how* these practices contribute to or inhibit the variety of musical genres, moods, and emotions expressed in worship.

*Imagine* ways of expanding the congregation's capacity for hospitality, candor, and forbearance in making decisions about worship.

# Notes

PREFACE

1. Jane Rogers Vann, *Gathered before God: Worship-Centered Church Renewal* (Louisville, KY: Westminster John Knox Press, 2004).

2. Tom F. Driver, *Liberating Rites: Understanding the Transformative Power of Ritual* (Boulder, CO: Westview Press, 1998), 212. Originally published as *The Magic of Ritual: Our Need for Liberating Rites That Transform Our Lives and Our Communities* (San Francisco: HarperSanFrancisco, 1991).

3. Gilbert Ostdiek, *Catechesis for Liturgy: A Program for Parish Involvement* (Washington, DC: Pastoral Press, 1986), 89.

4. Ibid., the whole work.

5. Cornelius Plantinga Jr. and Sue A. Rozeboom, eds., *Discerning the Spirits: A Guide to Thinking about Christian Worship Today* (Grand Rapids: Wm. B. Eerdmans Pub. Co., 2003); Jonny Baker and Doug Gay, compilers, *Alternative Worship: Resources from and for the Emerging Church* (Grand Rapids: Baker Books, 2004); Ronald P. Byars, *The Future of Protestant Worship: Beyond the Worship Wars* (Louisville, KY: Westminster John Knox Press, 2002); Thomas G. Long, *Beyond the Worship Wars: Building Vital and Faithful Worship* (Bethesda, MD: Alban Institute, 2001).

CHAPTER 1: NOT TALKING ABOUT WORSHIP

1. Edward Anders Sovik [Sövik], *Architecture for Worship* (Minneapolis: Augsburg Pub. House, 1973), 46.

2. Augsburg Confession, art. 7, in *The Book of Concord: The Confessions of the Evangelical Lutheran Church*, ed. Robert Kolb and Timothy J. Wengert, trans. Charles Arand (Minneapolis: Fortress Press, 2000), 42. Similar language is used in Presbyterian documents.

3. Presbyterian Church (U.S.A.) [PC(USA)], *Book of Common Worship* (Louisville, KY: Westminster/John Knox Press, 1993), 13.

CHAPTER 2: THE SYMBOLIC LANGUAGES OF WORSHIP

1. Gordon W. Lathrop, *Holy Things: A Liturgical Theology* (Minneapolis: Fortress Press, 1993), 95.

2. Don E. Saliers, *Worship and Spirituality*, 2nd ed. (Akron, OH: Order of Saint Luke Pubs., 1996), 6.

133

3. Ibid., 8.

4. Craig Dykstra, "A Way of Seeing: Imagination and the Pastoral Life," *Christian Century* 125 (April 8, 2008): 26.

5. Quoted in L. Gregory Jones, "Learning Curve," *Christian Century* 124 (August 7, 2007): 33.

6. Ronald P. Byars, *Lift Your Hearts on High: Eucharistic Prayer in the Reformed Tradition* (Louisville, KY: Westminster John Knox Press, 2005), xiv.

7. Saliers, *Worship and Spirituality*, 29.

8. Ibid., 31; also see Ostdiek, *Catechesis for Liturgy*; and Don E. Saliers, *Worship as Theology: Foretaste of Glory Divine* (Nashville: Abingdon Press, 1994).

9. Saliers, *Worship and Spirituality*, 29–30.

10. Louis K. Dupré, *Symbols of the Sacred* (Grand Rapids: Wm. B. Eerdmans Pub. Co., 2000), 2.

11. PC(USA), Directory for Worship, in *Constitution of the Presbyterian Church (U.S.A.)*, pt. 2, *Book of Order, 2007–2009* (Louisville, KY: Office of the General Assembly, PC(USA), 2007), W-1.1003.

12. Saliers, *Worship and Spirituality*, 33.

13. Ibid., 32.

14. Ronald P. Byars, "Body Language," *Call to Worship: Liturgy, Music, Preaching, and the Arts* 35 (2001): 4–5.

15. Office of Theology and Worship, PC(USA), *Invitation to Christ: A Guide to Sacramental Practices* (Louisville, KY: PC(USA), 2006), 10–12.

16. Ibid., 11.

17. Steve Shussett, "Embodied Spirituality: Is There Any Body in Worship?" *Call to Worship: Liturgy, Music, Preaching, and the Arts* 38 (2004): 11.

18. Ibid., 13.

19. Lathrop, *Holy Things*, 10–11.

20. Daniel T. Benedict, *Patterned by Grace: How Liturgy Shapes Us* (Nashville: Upper Room Books, 2007), 124.

21. Ibid., 124–25.

22. Ibid., 16.

23. Jean [John] Calvin, *Short Treatise on the Holy Supper of Our Lord and Only Savior Jesus Christ* (1541), in his *Theological Treatises*, trans. J. K. S. Reid, Library of Christian Classics 22 (Philadelphia: Westminster Press, 1954), 143–44; quoted in James White, *Documents of Christian Worship: Descriptive and Interpretive Sources* (Louisville, KY: Westminster/John Knox Press, 1992), 203.

24. Ronald P. Byars, *Christian Worship: Glorifying and Enjoying God* (Louisville, KY: Geneva Press, 2000), 31.

CHAPTER 3: GATHERING GOD'S PEOPLE

1. D. Foy Christopherson, *A Place of Encounter: Renewing Worship Spaces* (Minneapolis: Augsburg Fortress, 2004), 14.

2. Peter Hammond, *Liturgy and Architecture* (London: Barrie & Rockliff, 1960), 9.

3. Ostdiek, *Catechesis for Liturgy*, 76.

4. Robert Hovda, "It Begins with the Assembly," in *Environment for Worship: A Reader*, ed. Secretariat, Bishops' Committee on the Liturgy, National Conference of Catholic Bishops

and the Center for Pastoral Liturgy, Catholic University of America (Washington, DC: U.S. Catholic Conference, 1980), 37.

5. Ostdiek, *Catechesis for Liturgy*, 69.

6. Long, *Beyond the Worship Wars*, chap. 6.

7. Christopherson, *Place of Encounter*, 33.

8. Evangelical Lutheran Church in America [ELCA], *Principles for Worship* (Minneapolis: Augsburg Fortress, 2002), 69.

9. United Church of Christ [UCC], *Book of Worship* (Cleveland: Local Church Ministries, United Church Press, 2006), 18.

10. Mark A. Torgerson, *An Architecture of Immanence: Architecture for Worship and Ministry Today* (Grand Rapids: Wm. B. Eerdmans Pub. Co., 2007), 9.

11. Richard S. Vosko, "Introduction," in *Architecture for the Gods*, by Michael J. Crosbie (New York: Watson-Guptill Pubs., 2000), 8.

12. Ibid., 9.

13. Saliers, *Worship as Theology*, 49.

14. Ostdiek, *Catechesis for Liturgy*, 84.

15. ELCA, *Principles for Worship*, 91.

16. Ostdiek, *Catechesis for Liturgy*, 76.

17. Christopherson, *Place of Encounter*, 53.

18. PC(USA), "Directory for Worship," W-1.3021.

19. ELCA, *Principles for Worship*, 88.

20. Ibid., 89.

21. Ibid., 90.

22. Sara Webb Phillips, "The Role of Artists in Worship," in *Worship Matters: A United Methodist Guide to Worship Work*, ed. E. Byron Anderson (Nashville: Discipleship Resources, 1999), 1:164.

## CHAPTER 4: DRESSING THE SPACE

1. William A. Dyrness, *Visual Faith: Art, Theology, and Worship in Dialogue* (Grand Rapids: Baker Academic, 2001), 94.

2. Robin M. Jensen, *The Substance of Things Seen: Art, Faith, and the Christian Community* (Grand Rapids: Wm. B. Eerdmans Pub. Co., 2004).

3. Ibid., 2.

4. Thomas Matthews, *The Clash of the Gods: A Reinterpretation of Early Christian Art* (Princeton, NJ: Princeton University Press, 1993), 11; cited in William A. Dyrness, *Reformed Theology and Visual Culture: The Protestant Imagination from Calvin to Edwards* (New York: Cambridge University Press, 2004), 301.

5. Jensen, *Substance of Things Seen*, 8.

6. Ibid., 8–9.

7. James F. White and Susan J. White, *Church Architecture: Building and Renovating for Christian Worship* (Nashville: Abingdon Press, 1988), 155–57.

8. Jensen, *Substance of Things Seen*, 133.

9. Ostdiek, *Catechesis for Liturgy*, 49.

10. Dupré, *Symbols of the Sacred*, 3.

11. Ibid.

12. Dyrness, *Visual Faith*, 156.

13. Ibid.

14. Don E. Saliers, *Worship Come to Its Senses* (Nashville: Abingdon Press, 1996), 14–15.

15. Andrew M. Greeley, *The Catholic Myth: The Behavior and Beliefs of American Catholics* (New York: Scribner, 1990), 4; cited in Eileen D. Crowley, *Liturgical Art for a Media Culture* (Collegeville, MN: Liturgical Press, 2007), 52.

16. For a more thorough exploration of these issues, see Crowley, *Liturgical Art*, 37–58, on which this section depends.

17. Ibid., 78.

18. PC(USA), "Directory for Worship," W-1.3034.

19. ELCA, *Principles for Worship*, 72.

20. UCC, *Book of Worship*, 19.

21. ELCA, *Principles for Worship*, 73.

22. UCC, *Book of Worship*, 18.

23. In naming what might obscure the gospel, the Roman Catholic documents rule out anything "trivial, fake, cheap, shoddy, or superficial." Following this guideline calls for careful attention to detail. For example, Roman Catholic churches do not allow artificial flowers for weddings. See Bishops' Committee on the Liturgy, National Council of Catholic Bishops, *Environment and Art in Catholic Worship* (Washington, DC: U.S. Catholic Conference, 1978).

24. Crowley, *Liturgical Art for a Media Culture*, 80.

25. Ibid., 93. For detailed suggestions for media ministries, see her chapter "Frameworks for Evaluation of Media in Worship," 59–88.

26. "We as churches must work hard to win back artists whom we have alienated for so long," writes Hovda in "It Begins with the Assembly," 39.

27. Christopherson, *Place of Encounter*, 67.

28. Frank Burch Brown, *Good Taste, Bad Taste, and Christian Taste: Aesthetics in Religious Life* (New York: Oxford University Press, 2000), 250–51.

29. UCC, *Book of Worship*, "Introduction," 16.

30. ELCA, *Principles for Worship*, 72.

31. Ibid.

## CHAPTER 5: ENACTING WORSHIP

1. Craig Douglas Erickson, *Participating in Worship: History, Theory, and Practice* (Louisville, KY: Westminster/John Knox Press, 1989), 151.

2. Hovda, "It Begins with the Assembly," 41.

3. Robert E. Webber, *Worship Is a Verb: Eight Principles for Transforming Worship*, 2nd ed. (Peabody, MA: Hendrickson Publishers, 1992), 2.

4. Don E. Saliers, "The Power of Sign-Acts," in Anderson, *Worship Matters*, 1:175.

5. Byron D. Stuhlman, *Prayer Book Rubrics Expanded* (New York: Church Publishing, 1987), 21.

6. ELCA, *Principles for Worship*, 7.

7. Byars, "Body Language," 4–5.

8. Kathryn Sparks, "Embodied Prayer: Reclaiming the Age-Old Wisdom of the Body through Movement and Dance," *Call to Worship: Liturgy, Music, Preaching, and the Arts* 40 (2007): 16; quoting Jürgen Moltmann, *God in Creation* (Minneapolis: Fortress Press, 1993), 256; and Mary T. Prokes, *Toward a Theology of the Body* (Grand Rapids: Wm. B. Eerdmans Pub. Co., 1996), 259.

9. Kendra G. Hotz and Matthew T. Mathews, *Shaping the Christian Life: Worship and the Religious Affections* (Louisville, KY: Westminster John Knox Press, 2006), 138.

10. PC(USA), *Book of Common Worship*, 72.

11. Shussett, "Embodied Spirituality," 10–16.

12. Saliers, "The Power of Sign-Acts," 173.

13. Ibid.

14. PC(USA) published this as *Invitation to Christ*.

15. Erickson, *Participating in Worship*, 155–56.

16. Basil the Great, *De Spiritu Sancto* 27.66, in Sources chrétiennes 17:236–37; ET, *On the Holy Spirit* (Crestwood, NY: St. Vladimir's Seminary, 1980), 100; as quoted in Erickson, *Participating in Worship*, 159.

17. Erickson, *Participating in Worship*, 167.

18. Ibid., 163.

19. Ibid., 171.

20. Ibid., 30.

21. Saliers, "The Power of Sign-Acts," 1:175.

22. PC(USA), Directory for Worship, W-1.1004.

23. Rosalie Bent Branigan, "The Work of Liturgical Dancers," in Anderson, *Worship Matters*, 2:65.

24. Ibid., 69–70.

25. PC(USA), Directory for Worship, W-2.3003.

26. Ibid., W-2.3002.

27. Ibid., W-2.4001.

28. Ibid., W-2.4002.

29. Ibid., W-2.4001.

## CHAPTER 6: TIMEKEEPING

1. Laurence Hull Stookey, *Calendar: Christ's Time for the Church* (Nashville: Abingdon Press, 1996), 22, 29.

2. Ministry Unit on Theology and Worship, PC(USA), *Liturgical Year*, Supplemental Liturgical Resource 7 (Louisville, KY: Westminster/John Knox Press, 1991), 21.

3. Stookey, *Calendar*, 17.

4. Ibid.

5. Ibid., 19.

6. "Resources for the Liturgical Year," in *Companion to the Book of Common Worship*, ed. Peter C. Bower (Louisville, KY: Geneva Press and Office of Theology and Worship, PC(USA), 2003), 84.

7. Lathrop, *Holy Things*, 10–11.

8. Saliers, *Worship Come to Its Senses*, 19.

9. Ibid., 21.

10. For much of the material in this section, I am dependent on Peter C. Bower, *Companion to the Book of Common Worship*; and *Sundays and Seasons 2002* (Minneapolis: Augsburg Fortress, 2001).

11. F. Russell Mitman, *Worship in the Shape of Scripture* (Cleveland: Pilgrim Press, 2001), 10.

12. Bower, "Resources for the Liturgical Year," 93.

13. *Sundays and Seasons 2002*, 24.

14. Ibid., 106.

15. Ibid., 105–6.

16. See the prayer of commendation for the funeral service in PC(USA), *Book of Common Worship*, 925.

17. Bower, "Resources for the Liturgical Year," 110.

18. Ibid., 107.

19. Ibid., 118.

20. Ibid., 146–47.

21. Lathrop, *Holy Things*, 111–12.

22. PC(USA), "Directory for Worship," W-3.2002.

23. Ibid.

24. Ibid.

25. Ibid.

26. Ibid.

27. Ibid.

28. Ibid.

## CHAPTER 7: PROCLAIMING GOD'S PRAISE

1. Gail Ramshaw, *God beyond Gender: Feminist Christian God-Language* (Minneapolis: Fortress Press, 1995), 6.

2. Ronald P. Byars, *What Language Shall I Borrow? The Bible and Christian Worship* (Grand Rapids: Wm. B. Eerdmans Pub. Co., 2008), 5.

3. John H. Westerhoff, "Evangelism, Evangelization, and Catechesis: Defining Terms and Making the Case for Evangelization," *Call to Worship: Liturgy, Music, Preaching, and the Arts* 36 (2002–3): 5–14.

4. Marva A. Dawn, *A Royal Waste of Time: The Splendor of Worshiping God and Being Church for the World* (Grand Rapids: Wm. B. Eerdmans Pub. Co., 1999), 124.

5. Byars, *What Language Shall I Borrow?* xvi.

6. Ibid., xvii.

7. Mitman, *Worship in the Shape of Scripture*, 89. Mitman (89) contrasts God's attractiveness with current cultural alternatives: "Worship events shaped by the form of God's own self-revelation[,] instead of continually pandering to people's perception of their religious needs and focusing on the bad or good experiences of the human condition[,] will offer an inviting alternative to the hype [that] the culture turns up to sell its meaninglessness. . . . People tired of the culture's reruns will begin to overhear—perhaps even for the first time—the old, old story that seeks again to awaken those dozing in boredom and to revitalize the body that is Christ's in today's world." See also Mitman's analysis of biblical theophanies, whose structure is reflected in the liturgy (31–53).

8. PC(USA), Directory for Worship, W-1.2005.

9. Ostdiek, *Catechesis for Liturgy*, 156.

10. See Anderson, ed., *Worship Matters*, 2 vols.; Laurence Hull Stookey, *Let the Whole Church Say Amen! A Guide for Those Who Pray in Public* (Nashville: Abingdon Press, 2001); Bower, *Companion to the Book of Common Worship*; Craig Alan Satterlee, *Presiding in the Assembly: A Worship Handbook* (Minneapolis: Augsburg Fortress, 2003).

11. Ostdiek, *Catechesis for Liturgy*, 151.

12. William Sydnor, *Your Voice, God's Word: Reading the Bible in Church* (Harrisburg, PA: Morehouse Publishing, 1988), ix.

13. Ostdiek, *Catechesis for Liturgy*, 157.

14. Fred B. Craddock, *Overhearing the Gospel* (Nashville: Abingdon Press, 1978), 13.

15. Mitman, *Worship in the Shape of Scripture*, 56.

16. Gail Ramshaw, *Christ in Sacred Speech: The Meaning of Liturgical Language* (Philadelphia: Fortress Press, 1986), 7–8.

17. Mitman, *Worship in the Shape of Scripture*, 52.

18. See Stookey, *Let the Whole Church Say Amen!* See esp. "Exercise 13: Helping All to Feel Included."

19. Grant S. White, "The Work of Reading the Word in Public Worship," in Anderson, *Worship Matters*, 2:26.

20. J. Barrie Shepherd, *Whatever Happened to Delight? Preaching the Gospel in Poetry and Parables* (Louisville, KY: Westminster John Knox Press, 2006), 3.

21. Ibid., 61.

22. Craig Alan Satterlee, *When God Speaks through Change: Preaching in Times of Congregational Transition* (Herndon, VA: Alban Institute, 2005), 22.

23. Mitman, *Worship in the Shape of Scripture*, 56.

24. Shepherd, *Whatever Happened to Delight?* 78.

25. Lillian Daniel, *Tell It Like It Is: Reclaiming the Practice of Testimony* (Herndon, VA: Alban Institute, 2006), xiv.

26. Thomas G. Long, *Testimony: Talking Ourselves into Being Christian* (San Francisco: Jossey-Bass, 2004), xvii.

27. Daniel, *Tell It Like It Is*, 153.

28. ELCA, *Principles for Worship*, 12.

29. PC(USA), Directory for Worship, W-1.2005.

## CHAPTER 8: LIFTING OUR VOICES

1. Donald E. Saliers, "Singing Our Lives," in *Practicing Our Faith: A Way of Life for a Searching People*, ed. Dorothy C. Bass (San Francisco: Jossey-Bass, 1997), 183–84.

2. John XXIII, Bishop of Rome, Constitution on the Sacred Liturgy, in *Documents of Vatican II*, ed. Walter M. Abbott (New York: Guild Press, 1966), 144.

3. ELCA, *Principles for Worship*, 26.

4. Ibid., 28.

5. C. Michael Hawn, "Reverse Missions: Global Singing for Local Congregations," in *Music in Christian Worship: At the Service of the Liturgy*, ed. Charlotte Y. Kroeker (Collegeville, MN: Liturgical Press, 2005), 106.

6. Saliers, "Singing Our Lives," 182.

7. Donald E. Saliers, "Sounding the Symbols of Faith: Exploring the Nonverbal Languages of Christian Worship," in Kroeker, *Music in Christian Worship*, 17–26.

8. Ibid., 23.

9. Ibid., 23–24.

10. Ibid., 24.

11. Michael S. Driscoll, "Musical Mystagogy: Catechizing through the Sacred Arts," in Kroeker, *Music in Christian Worship*, 36.

12. Long, *Beyond the Worship Wars*, 61.

13. Linda J. Clark, Joanne Swenson, and Mark Stamm, *How We Seek God Together: Exploring Worship Style* (Bethesda, MD: Alban Institute, 2001), 15–16.

14. Ibid., 17–18.

15. PC(USA), Directory for Worship, W-2.1001.

16. Hawn, "Reverse Missions," in Kroeker, *Music in Christian Worship*, 107.

17. ELCA, *Principles for Worship*, 35.

18. John D. Witvliet, "We Are What We Sing," *Reformed Worship* 60 (June 2001): 6.

19. Ibid.

20. For the suggestions in this section, I depend on Clark et al., *How We Seek God Together*, 90–91.

21. Plantinga and Rozeboom, *Discerning the Spirits*, 5–7.

22. Ibid., 8.

23. Ibid., 9.

24. Ibid.

25. Ibid.

26. Paul Westermeyer, *The Church Musician*, rev. ed. (Minneapolis: Augsburg Fortress, 1997), 41.

27. ELCA, *Principles for Worship*, 26.

28. Ibid., 28.